A Call to Authentic Christian Living

The
Book of
James

Rev. Scot Saul

Table of Contents

The Book of James: A Study for Authentic Christian Living

Introduction to the Study of James

The Book of James is one of the most practical books in the New Testament, often called the "Proverbs of the New Testament" because of its wisdom-filled approach to Christian living. Written by James, the half-brother of Jesus, this letter provides a direct and uncompromising call to live out faith through action. Unlike Paul's epistles, which focus heavily on doctrine and theology, James' writing is deeply rooted in everyday life—challenging believers to live out their faith in tangible ways.

James was not always a believer. During Jesus' earthly ministry, James and his brothers were skeptical of Him *(John 7:5)*. However, after witnessing the resurrected Christ *(1 Corinthians 15:7)*, James became a devoted follower and a key leader in the early church in Jerusalem *(Acts 15:13-21)*. His letter reflects a deep concern for Christians who faced persecution and trials, encouraging them to remain steadfast and put their faith into practice.

This epistle is widely believed to be the earliest book of the New Testament, likely written between A.D. 44-49. Interestingly, James almost did not make it into the canon of Scripture due to its strong emphasis on works. Some early church leaders questioned how it aligned with Paul's teachings on grace. However, when viewed correctly, James did not contradict Paul but complemented his message: *while salvation comes by faith alone, true faith is always demonstrated through action.*

Key Themes to Explore

Throughout this study, we will delve into James' teachings on several core aspects of the Christian life:

- **Trials and Perseverance:** How hardships serve as opportunities for spiritual growth.

- **Faith in Action:** The importance of living out our faith through deeds rather than merely hearing the Word.

- **Wisdom and Speech:** How our words can build up or tear down, and the role of godly wisdom in our daily decisions.

- **Humility and Justice:** The call to care for those in need and to live without favoritism.

- **Wealth and Generosity:** A warning against the idolatry of wealth and the need for a kingdom-first mindset.

- **Prayer:** The power of prayer to transform our lives and communities.

Goals for This Study

By the end of this study, participants will be challenged to:

- **Consider Hardships as Opportunities:** Embrace trials as a means of spiritual maturity.

- **Align Actions with Faith:** Demonstrate their belief in Christ through tangible acts of obedience and service.

- **Speak with Wisdom:** Cultivate speech that reflects the grace and truth of Jesus.

- **Live with Humility:** Depend on God and extend compassion to those who are marginalized.

- **Prioritize Prayer:** Recognize prayer as a vital, ongoing part of every aspect of life.

Discussion Questions for the Introduction Session

1. **What Does It Mean to Live an Active Faith:** How does James challenge us to put our faith into practice rather than just listening to God's Word?

2. **Historical Context and Transformation:** Considering that James was once skeptical of Jesus, how does his personal transformation encourage you in your own faith journey?

3. **Faith and Works:** In what ways have you experienced the tension between merely hearing the Word and actively living it out? What challenges have you faced?

4. **The Relevance of James Today:** How do the practical teachings of James apply to our modern lives, especially in the face of personal trials and societal pressures?

Reflection and Commitment: Take a moment to reflect on these questions. Consider journaling your thoughts on what it means to have a faith that actively shapes your actions and decisions. How might this study challenge you to evaluate your own walk with God?

Closing Prayer

Heavenly Father,

Thank You for Your Word that challenges and transforms us. As we begin this journey through the Book of James, open our hearts to the truths You have for us. Help us to see our trials as opportunities for growth and to understand that true faith is not merely heard but lived out in love, wisdom, and obedience. May Your Spirit guide us in every step, and may we be doers of the Word, reflecting the character of Christ in all that we do. In Jesus' name, we pray. Amen.

Session 1

James 1:1–12 – What if we started considering our troubles "pure joy?"

As we begin our journey through the Book of James, we are immediately confronted with a challenging concept: counting our trials as joy. In a world that often views difficulties as setbacks, James invites us to view them as opportunities for growth and spiritual maturity. This session will help us understand how perseverance in the face of hardship leads to a faith that is refined and complete. Let us open our hearts to embrace God's perspective on suffering and find joy in the testing of our faith.

Session 1: James 1:1–12

- James 1:2–4: "Consider it pure joy…"
- James 1:5–8: "If any of you lacks wisdom…"
- James 1:12: "Blessed is the one who perseveres under trial…"

1 James, a servant of God and of the Lord Jesus Christ, To the twelve tribes scattered among the nations: Greetings. 2 Consider it pure joy, my brothers and sisters, whenever you face trials of many kinds, 3 because you know that the testing of your faith produces perseverance. 4 Let perseverance finish its work so that you may be mature and complete, not lacking anything. 5 If any of you lacks wisdom, you should ask God, who gives generously to all without finding fault, and it will be given to you. 6 But when you ask, you must believe and not doubt, because the one who doubts is like a

wave of the sea, blown and tossed by the wind. **7** That person should not expect to receive anything from the Lord. **8** Such a person is double-minded and unstable in all they do. **9** Believers in humble circumstances ought to take pride in their high position. **10** But the rich should take pride in their humiliation—since they will pass away like a wild flower. **11** For the sun rises with scorching heat and withers the plant; its blossom falls, and its beauty is destroyed. In the same way, the rich will fade away even while they go about their business. **12** Blessed is the one who perseveres under trial because, having stood the test, that person will receive the crown of life that the Lord has promised to those who love him.

James 1:2–4 – "Consider it pure joy…"

How does our faith grow stronger through hardships?

- **Growth Through Perseverance:** Trials are opportunities that build perseverance—a quality that helps us mature spiritually. Just as physical muscles grow stronger with exercise, our faith is refined and strengthened when we endure difficulties.

Romans 5:3-5 – "Not only so, but we also glory in our sufferings, because we know that suffering produces perseverance; perseverance, character; and character, hope."

- **Dependence on God:** Hardships force us to lean on God rather than on our own strength. This dependence deepens our relationship with Him as we learn to trust His guidance and care.

Proverbs 3:5-6 – "Trust in the Lord with all your heart and lean not on your own understanding; in all your ways submit to him, and he will make your paths straight."

- **Character Formation:** Difficult times cultivate qualities like patience, resilience, and empathy, traits that shape a deeper, more grounded faith. Overcoming challenges shapes our character and aligns us more closely with Christ's example.

1 Peter 1:6-7 – "In all this you greatly rejoice, though now for a little while you may have had to suffer grief in all kinds of trials... These have come so that the proven genuineness of your faith—of greater worth than gold...—may result in praise, glory and honor when Jesus Christ is revealed."

James 1:5–8 – "If any of you lacks wisdom…"

Why is it important to seek God's wisdom during trials, and how does doubt affect our request for wisdom?

- **Access to Divine Guidance:** When we ask God for wisdom, we invite His guidance into our lives. His wisdom helps us navigate complex and challenging situations in a way that reflects His truth.

Proverbs 2:6 – "For the Lord gives wisdom; from his mouth come knowledge and understanding."

- **Importance of Faith:** The passage emphasizes asking "without doubting." Faith that is steadfast opens the door for God to work in our lives, while doubt leads to instability and prevents us from fully receiving His wisdom.

Matthew 21:21-22 – "...if you believe, you will receive whatever you ask for in prayer. ... And whatever you ask for in prayer, you will receive, if you have faith."

- **Overcoming Double-mindedness:** A double-minded approach (being indecisive or wavering) undermines our ability to trust and act on God's guidance. Cultivating a single-minded focus on God strengthens our resolve during trials. Being resolute in our faith prevents double-mindedness and allows us to benefit from God's wisdom fully.

James 1:6 – "But when you ask, you must believe and not doubt..."

James 1:12 – "Blessed is the one who perseveres under trial..."

What does it mean to persevere through trials, and what promise is attached to this perseverance?

- **Endurance as a Mark of Faith:** Perseverance means continuing in faith despite difficulties, trusting that God is using these experiences to shape and refine us.

Hebrews 12:1-2 – "...let us run with perseverance the race marked out for us, fixing our eyes on Jesus, the pioneer and perfecter of faith."

- **Spiritual Reward:** The promise attached to perseverance is the "crown of life" that God has promised to those who love Him. This symbolizes eternal reward and the ultimate vindication of our faithfulness.

Revelation 2:10 – "Be faithful, even to the point of death, and I will give you life as your victor's crown."

- **Building a Resilient Faith:** Each trial overcome reinforces our confidence in God's provision and care, making our faith more robust and resilient for future challenges.

Romans 8:18 – "I consider that our present sufferings are not worth comparing with the glory that will be revealed in us."

Session 1 - Key Summary Points

1. **James 1:2–4 – "Consider it pure joy..."**

- Trials are not meaningless; they test and strengthen our faith.
- Perseverance develops spiritual depth and character, making us complete in Christ.
- Instead of resisting trials, believers should embrace them with joy, knowing they lead to endurance and character growth.

2. **James 1:5–8 – "If any of you lacks wisdom..."**

- Wisdom is essential to navigate trials with faith and understanding.
- God gives wisdom generously to those who ask in faith without doubting.
- A double-minded person (wavering between faith and doubt) struggles to receive from God.

3. **James 1:12 – "Blessed is the one who perseveres under trial..."**

- Those who endure trials faithfully will receive God's blessing and the crown of life.
- Perseverance in faith proves our love for God.
- Eternal reward awaits those who remain steadfast under hardship.

A. Trials Reveal the Depth of Our Faith

Challenges test what we really believe. When life is hard, we find out if our trust is in God—or in our comfort, routine, or resources. Hardships expose our foundations, and they deepen our dependence on the Lord.

Cross-reference: 1 Peter 1:6–7 – Trials refine faith like gold, proving its genuineness.

B. Endurance Builds Spiritual Maturity

As we persevere through suffering, we don't just survive—we grow. James says perseverance must finish its work so we may be "mature and complete, not lacking anything." God uses difficulties as training grounds for our souls—building spiritual endurance, patience, and character.

Cross-reference: Romans 5:3–5 – "Suffering produces perseverance; perseverance, character; and character, hope."

C. God Offers Wisdom in the Storm

James 1:5 reminds us that when we seek wisdom, God gives it freely – as long as we trust Him fully. We may not always get answers to *why*, but He gives direction for *what to do next*. Trials become places where we hear God most clearly if we listen.

Cross-reference: Proverbs 3:5–6 – Trust in the Lord and He will direct your paths.

D. The Joy Isn't in the Pain, but in the Purpose

James doesn't ask us to enjoy suffering but to find joy in what suffering can produce. We rejoice because we know God is doing something in us, not because the trial itself feels good.

Cross-reference: Hebrews 12:11 – "No discipline seems pleasant at the time... but later it produces a harvest of righteousness."

E. Endurance Leads to Blessing

James 1:12 promises that those who persevere under trial will receive the crown of life. God honors endurance—not just for survival, but because it's an expression of love and loyalty toward Him.

Cross-reference: 2 Corinthians 4:17 – "Our light and momentary troubles are achieving for us an eternal glory that far outweighs them all."

Closing Question:

"How can you shift your perspective to see trials as opportunities for growth rather than obstacles to avoid?"

Challenge

- What trial are you facing that you can begin to view differently—with a perspective of growth and trust?
- Ask God for wisdom in one specific hardship you're facing this week—and look for His response.

Struggle: Finding joy in trials.

Practical Steps:

- Keep a gratitude journal to recognize God's work in tough times.
- Pray daily for wisdom and endurance.
- Seek encouragement from mature believers.

Conclusion:

The journey of faith is not about avoiding trials but about learning to endure them with God's wisdom and strength. James reminds us that trials refine our faith, making us mature and complete. However, perseverance alone is not enough—we must seek God's wisdom to navigate challenges in a way that glorifies Him. When we lack wisdom, God promises to give it generously when we ask in faith.

As we face difficulties, let's remember that our faith must rest in God, not our circumstances. Instead of being tossed by the winds of doubt, let's anchor ourselves in the unshakable truth of God's character. He is faithful, and He will guide us through every storm.

Key Reflection:

Are we asking for wisdom with confidence, fully trusting that God will lead us through our trials? Let's commit to praying for wisdom and choosing joy, knowing that every challenge is an opportunity to grow in faith.

Closing Prayer:

Heavenly Father, thank You for reminding us that trials are not punishments but pathways to maturity. Help us to count it all joy when we face difficulties, knowing You are producing endurance in us. Strengthen our faith and give us wisdom to see through Your eyes. May we trust You in every circumstance, believing You are shaping us for Your glory. In Jesus' name, Amen.

Session 2

James 1:13–18 – How does your relationship with God grow and soar when you trust Him?

Temptation is an inevitable part of life, but the source of temptation is never from God. In this session, we will learn to recognize the difference between the tests God allows for our growth and the temptations that arise from our own desires. James reminds us that every good and perfect gift comes from above. Let us reflect on how our relationship with God deepens when we trust Him fully and reject the deception of sin.

Session 2: James 1:13–18

- James 1:13–15: "When tempted, no one should say…"
- James 1:16–18: "Every good and perfect gift is from above…"

13 When tempted, no one should say, "God is tempting me." For God cannot be tempted by evil, nor does he tempt anyone; **14** but each person is tempted when they are dragged away by their own evil desire and enticed. **15** Then, after desire has conceived, it gives birth to sin; and sin, when it is full-grown, gives birth to death. **16** Don't be deceived, my dear brothers and sisters. **17** Every good and perfect gift is from above, coming down from the Father of the heavenly lights, who does not change like shifting shadows. **18** He chose to give us birth through the word of truth, that we might be a kind of first fruits of all he created.

James 1:13–15 – "When tempted, no one should say…"

What are some practical ways to recognize and resist temptation before it leads to sin?

- **Be Aware of Personal Weaknesses:** Temptation often begins in areas where we are most vulnerable. Recognizing personal weaknesses helps us stay on guard.

1st Corinthians 10:13 – "No temptation has overtaken you except what is common to mankind. And God is faithful; he will not let you be tempted beyond what you can bear."

- **Acknowledge the Source of Temptation:** Temptation comes from our own desires, not from God. When we grasp this, we stop blaming God and start turning to Him for the help we truly need.
- *Galatians 5:16 – "So I say, walk by the Spirit, and you will not gratify the desires of the flesh."*
- **Be Mindful of Triggers and Weaknesses:** Identifying what situations, thoughts, or influences lead us into temptation can help us avoid them.

Proverbs 4:23 – "Above all else, guard your heart, for everything you do flows from it."

- **Replace Temptation with Godly Pursuits:** Instead of focusing on what tempts us, we should fill our hearts and minds with things that draw us closer to God.

Colossians 3:2 – "Set your minds on things above, not on earthly things."

- **Use Scripture as a Weapon:** Jesus resisted temptation by using Scripture. When faced with temptation, we should recall and apply God's Word.

Ephesians 6:17 – "Take the helmet of salvation and the sword of the Spirit, which is the word of God."

- **Seek Accountability and Prayer:** Having trusted believers who can pray for and encourage us in our struggles can help us stay strong.

Ecclesiastes 4:9-10 – *"Two are better than one... If either of them falls down, one can help the other up."*

James 1:16–18 – "Every good and perfect gift is from above..."

How does recognizing God as the giver of all good things change our perspective on life's blessings and challenges?

- **Fosters Gratitude Instead of Entitlement:** When we recognize that all good things come from God, we become more grateful and less entitled.

Psalm 107:1 – *"Give thanks to the Lord, for he is good; his love endures forever."*

- **Encourages Trust in God's Provision:** Knowing that God is the ultimate provider helps us trust Him, even in difficult times.

Matthew 7:11 – *"If you, then, though you are evil, know how to give good gifts to your children, how much more will your Father in heaven give good gifts to those who ask him!"*

- **Shifts Our Focus from Material to Spiritual Blessings:** We begin to see God's gifts not just in material things but in peace, wisdom, love, and salvation.

Ephesians 1:3 – "Praise be to the God and Father of our Lord Jesus Christ, who has blessed us in the heavenly realms with every spiritual blessing in Christ."

- **Helps Us See Challenges as Opportunities for Growth:** If every good gift is from God, even trials can be seen as opportunities to grow in faith.

Romans 8:28 – "And we know that in all things God works for the good of those who love him, who have been called according to his purpose."

- **Reminds Us to Give Freely as We Have Received:** When we acknowledge God as the giver, we are more willing to bless others with what we have.

2nd Corinthians 9:8 – "And God is able to bless you abundantly, so that in all things at all times, having all that you need, you will abound in every good work."

Session 2 - Key Summary Points

1. **James 1:13–15 – "When tempted, no one should say…"**

- God does not tempt anyone; temptation comes from our own desires.
- Sin begins with desire, which leads to sin when acted upon and ultimately results in death.

- We must take responsibility for our choices and resist sinful desires before they grow.

2. **James 1:16–18 – "Every good and perfect gift is from above..."**

- God is the source of all good things and never changes in His goodness.
- Unlike temptation, which leads to death, God gives life and every perfect gift.
- As believers, we are born again through God's truth, set apart as His special people.

A. God Doesn't Tempt Us—He Rescues Us

Trusting God begins with knowing His character is good and unchanging.

Temptation doesn't come from God. He is not trying to trip us up—He wants to grow us up.

When Christians believe that, they begin to walk in confidence rather than shame or fear.

Cross-reference: 1 Corinthians 10:13 – "God is faithful; He will not let you be tempted beyond what you can bear."

B. Trust Transforms Our Response to Temptation

When we trust God, we stop blaming Him and start resisting sin with His help.

Instead of giving in to desire (which James says leads to death), we learn to ask for strength and look for the way out.

Cross-reference: Psalm 119:11 – "I have hidden Your word in my heart that I might not sin against You."

C. Every Good Gift Comes from God

All the truly good things in our lives—love, joy, peace, provision—**are gifts from a generous Father.**

Trusting Him shifts our focus from what we don't have to what we've already received.

Cross-reference: Matthew 7:11 – "If you... know how to give good gifts... how much more will your Father in heaven give good things..."

D. God Is Steady When Life Isn't

James says God "does not change like shifting shadows." Trusting Him means **we anchor our lives to Someone who never changes, even when everything else does.**

Cross-reference: Hebrews 13:8 – "Jesus Christ is the same yesterday and today and forever."

E. Our New Identity Is Rooted in His Truth

James 1:18 says we were given new birth through the word of truth.

Trusting God means believing we are **born of His truth**, not defined by our past mistakes or present temptations.

Cross-reference: 2 Corinthians 5:17 – "If anyone is in Christ, he is a new creation..."

Closing Question

"In what areas of your life do you need to trust more in God's goodness rather than being drawn away by your own desires?"

Challenge

- Think of one recent moment of temptation or discouragement.
- How would that moment have changed if you had reminded yourself of God's goodness and provision?
- This week, write down three "good and perfect gifts" you've received from God. Let that reminder shape your trust.

Struggle: Resisting temptation.

Practical Steps:

- Identify triggers and replace harmful habits with godly practices.
- Memorize scripture that reinforces resisting sin.
- Find an accountability partner.

Conclusion:

James challenges us to see wealth and hardship through the lens of eternity. Whether rich or poor, our true value is found in our identity in Christ, not in our earthly status. Wealth fades, hardships pass, but the one who remains faithful to God receives the crown of life.

Likewise, temptation is a reality we all face. However, James reminds us that temptation is not from God but from the desires within us. When we let sin take root, it leads to death—but when we rely on God, He leads us into life.

Key Reflection:

Are we defining ourselves by earthly success or eternal treasures? Are we recognizing and resisting temptation, knowing that every good and perfect gift comes from our heavenly Father? Let's walk forward with contentment, humility, and vigilance, trusting in God's perfect plan for our lives.

Closing Prayer:

Lord God, we thank You for being the giver of every good and perfect gift. Help us recognize temptation for what it is and never doubt Your goodness. Teach us to trust in Your truth, not the deceits of the enemy. Keep us grounded in Your Word and lead us away from temptation and into a deeper relationship with You. In Christ's name, Amen.

Session 3

James 1:19–27 – How are you living out your faith?

Faith is not a passive belief but an active pursuit of righteousness. James calls us to be "doers of the Word, and not hearers only." In this session, we will explore the vital connection between hearing God's Word and living it out in practical ways. It's not enough to simply know the truth; we must embody it. Let's challenge ourselves to put our faith into action, making a real difference in the world around us.

Session 3: James 1:19–27

- James 1:19–21: "Everyone should be quick to listen…"
- James 1:22–25: "Do not merely listen to the word…"
- James 1:26–27: "Religion that God our Father accepts as pure…"

19 My dear brothers and sisters, take note of this: Everyone should be quick to listen, slow to speak and slow to become angry, **20** because human anger does not produce the righteousness that God desires. **21** Therefore, get rid of all moral filth and the evil that is so prevalent and humbly accept the word planted in you, which can save you. **22** Do not merely listen to the word, and so deceive yourselves. Do what it says. **23** Anyone who listens to the word but does not do what it says is like someone who looks at his face in a mirror **24** and, after looking at himself, goes away and immediately forgets what he looks like. **25** But whoever looks intently into the perfect law that gives freedom, and continues in it—not forgetting what they have heard, but doing it—they will be blessed in what they do. **26** Those who consider themselves religious and yet do not keep a tight rein on their tongues deceive themselves, and their religion is worthless. **27** Religion that God our Father accepts as pure and faultless is this: to look after orphans and widows in their distress and to keep oneself from being polluted by the world.

James 1:19–21 – "Everyone should be quick to listen..."

How does being quick to listen and slow to speak help us reflect Christ in our daily interactions?

- **Promotes Understanding:** Active listening allows us to understand others deeply, fostering empathy and reducing conflicts.

Proverbs 18:13 – "To answer before listening— that is folly and shame."

Philippians 2:4 – "Not looking to your own interests but each of you to the interests of the others."

- **Reflects Christ's Humility:** It mirrors the humility and gentleness of Christ, who listens and responds with love.

Matthew 11:29 – "Take my yoke upon you and learn from me, for I am gentle and humble in heart, and you will find rest for your souls."

James 3:17 – "But the wisdom that comes from heaven is first of all pure; then peace-loving, considerate, submissive, full of mercy and good fruit, impartial and sincere."

- **Prevents Misunderstandings:** Thoughtful speech minimizes misunderstandings and helps build trust in relationships.

Proverbs 15:1 – "A gentle answer turns away wrath, but a harsh word stirs up anger."

Colossians 4:6 – "Let your conversation be always full of grace, seasoned with salt, so that you may know how to answer everyone."

James 1:22–25 – "Do not merely listen to the word…"

What are some ways we can put God's Word into action in our daily lives?

- **Practical Application:** Identify specific actions that reflect biblical principles—such as acts of kindness, honesty, and service.

Matthew 5:16 – "In the same way, let your light shine before others, that they may see your good deeds and glorify your Father in heaven."

Galatians 6:9–10 – "Let us not become weary in doing good, for at the proper time we will reap a harvest if we do not give up. Therefore, as we have opportunity, let us do good to all people, especially to those who belong to the family of believers."

- **Intentional Living:** Set daily goals to live out Scripture, whether through personal discipline or serving others in your community.

Colossians 3:17 – "And whatever you do, whether in word or deed, do it all in the name of the Lord Jesus, giving thanks to God the Father through him."

James 2:17 – "In the same way, faith by itself, if it is not accompanied by action, is dead."

- **Ongoing Self-Examination:** Regularly reflect on your actions versus your beliefs to ensure alignment with God's commands.

2nd Corinthians 13:5 – "Examine yourselves to see whether you are in the faith; test yourselves. Do you not realize that Christ Jesus is in you—unless, of course, you fail the test?"

Psalm 139:23–24 – "Search me, God, and know my heart; test me and know my anxious thoughts. See if there is any offensive way in me, and lead me in the way everlasting."

James 1:26–27 – "Religion that God our Father accepts as pure..."

How does caring for the vulnerable (e.g., widows and orphans) reflect true faith? What are practical ways to live out this teaching?

- **Active Compassion:** True religion is seen in the way we care for those in need, showing God's love in tangible ways.

Proverbs 19:17 – "Whoever is kind to the poor lends to the Lord, and he will reward them for what they have done."

1st John 3:17–18 – "If anyone has material possessions and sees a brother or sister in need but has no pity on them, how can the love of God be in that person? Dear children, let us not love with words or speech but with actions and in truth."

- **Community Engagement:** Practical acts include volunteering, supporting charities, or simply being a consistent presence for those who are struggling.

Matthew 25:35–36 – "For I was hungry and you gave me something to eat, I was thirsty and you gave me something to drink, I was a stranger and you invited me in, I needed clothes and you clothed me, I was sick and you looked after me, I was in prison and you came to visit me."

Hebrews 13:16 – "And do not forget to do good and to share with others, for with such sacrifices God is pleased."

- **Personal Sacrifice:** Truly loving others often means setting aside our own comfort, convenience, or preferences so that others can receive compassion, fairness, and dignity—just as God calls us to do.*Luke 10:33–35 – "But a Samaritan, as he traveled, came where the man was; and when he saw him, he took pity on him. He went to him and bandaged his wounds, pouring on oil and wine. Then he put the man on his own donkey, brought him to an inn and took care of him."*

Philippians 2:4 – "Not looking to your own interests but each of you to the interests of the others."

Session 3 - Key Summary Points

1. **James 1:19–21 – "Everyone should be quick to listen…"**

- Believers should be **quick to listen, slow to speak, and slow to become angry** because human anger does not reflect God's righteousness.
- Removing moral filth and humbly accepting God's Word leads to spiritual transformation.
- True wisdom comes from listening and applying God's truth rather than reacting impulsively.

2. **James 1:22–25 – "Do not merely listen to the word…"**

- Hearing God's Word without action is **self-deception**; true faith is demonstrated through obedience.
- The Bible is like a mirror—showing us who we are—but it only benefits us if we respond to it.

3. Those who actively **live out God's Word** will experience His blessing.

4. **James 1:26–27 – "Religion that God our Father accepts as pure…"**

- True religion is not just words but a life of **self-control, compassion, and holiness**.
- Controlling one's **tongue** is a mark of genuine faith.
- Caring for **widows and orphans** and remaining **unstained by the world** reflects a heart aligned with God.

A. False Assurance Without Transformation

We deceive ourselves when we believe that simply attending church, reading Scripture, or hearing sermons is enough. Real faith transforms behavior—**obedience is the evidence** of understanding. Listening without acting creates a false sense of spiritual growth.

Cross-reference: Matthew 7:24–27 – The wise builder acts on Jesus' words, the foolish one does not.

B. Neglecting Personal Responsibility

Hearing God's truth places a **responsibility on us to respond**. When we ignore conviction or delay obedience, we deceive ourselves into thinking we're growing when we're really staying stagnant.

Cross-reference: Hebrews 4:12 – God's Word is living and active; it exposes and calls for a response.

C. Outward Religion Without Inward Change

We may appear religious—knowing verses and using Christian language—but **if we don't let God's Word reshape our hearts and actions**, especially in how we treat others, we're fooling ourselves.

Cross-reference: 1 Samuel 15:22 – "To obey is better than sacrifice."

Closing Question:

"In what ways can you be more intentional about not just hearing God's Word but actively living it out in your daily life?"

Challenge

- What is one command or truth from Scripture you've heard recently that you haven't acted on yet?
- What does it look like for you to **live out your faith** at school, at work, or at home?

Struggle: Being hearers but not doers of the Word.

Practical Steps:

- Set specific goals for action after reading scripture.
- Journal about ways to apply biblical truths in daily life.
- Volunteer in ministries that align with biblical principles.

Conclusion:

James makes it clear that faith is more than knowledge—it requires action. It's not enough to simply hear God's Word; we must obey it and let it transform us. Just as a mirror reveals what we look like,

Scripture reveals the condition of our hearts. The question is: *What will we do with what we see?*

True faith controls the tongue, cares for the vulnerable, and pursues holiness. If our faith does not move us toward compassionate action and righteous living, we must examine whether we are truly living out the Gospel.

Key Reflection:

Are we **active doers** of the Word, or are we just hearers? Let's take time this week to apply what God is teaching us—**whether in our speech, our service, or our personal holiness**—so that our faith reflects Christ to the world.

Closing Prayer:

Father, may we not only hear Your Word but live it. Help us to listen carefully, speak graciously, and act justly. Teach us to care for those in need and to keep our hearts pure before You. Thank You for showing us what true religion looks like. Empower us by Your Spirit to live it out every day. In Jesus' name, Amen.

Session 4

James 2:1–13 – How are you caring for those who don't normally get special attention?

The early church faced many challenges, but one of the most pervasive was the temptation of favoritism. James warns us against showing partiality based on outward appearances and calls us to reflect Christ's love for all people. In this session, we will discuss how we can embody God's love through our actions, treating everyone with dignity and respect. Let us be reminded that God's kingdom is one of equality, and in His eyes, everyone matters.

Session 4: James 2:1–13

- James 2:1–7: "My brothers and sisters, believers in our glorious Lord…"
- James 2:8–13: "If you really keep the royal law found in Scripture…

1 My brothers and sisters, believers in our glorious Lord Jesus Christ must not show favoritism. 2 Suppose a man comes into your meeting wearing a gold ring and fine clothes, and a poor man in filthy old clothes also comes in. 3 If you show special attention to the man wearing fine clothes and say, "Here's a good seat for you," but say to the poor man, "You stand there" or "Sit on the floor by my feet," 4 have you not discriminated among yourselves and become judges with evil thoughts? 5 Listen, my dear brothers and sisters: Has not God chosen those who are poor in the eyes of the world to be rich in faith and to inherit the kingdom he promised those who love him? 6

But you have dishonored the poor. Is it not the rich who are exploiting you? Are they not the ones who are dragging you into court? **7** Are they not the ones who are blaspheming the noble name of him to whom you belong? **8** If you really keep the royal law found in Scripture, "Love your neighbor as yourself," you are doing right. **9** But if you show favoritism, you sin and are convicted by the law as lawbreakers. **10** For whoever keeps the whole law and yet stumbles at just one point is guilty of breaking all of it. **11** For he who said, "You shall not commit adultery," also said, "You shall not murder." If you do not commit adultery but do commit murder, you have become a lawbreaker. **12** Speak and act as those who are going to be judged by the law that gives freedom, **13** because judgment without mercy will be shown to anyone who has not been merciful. Mercy triumphs over judgment.

James 2:1–7 – "Believers in our glorious Lord must not show favoritism…"

How does favoritism or prejudice show up in the church today?

- **Social or Economic Bias:** Some churches give preferential treatment to wealthier members, influential leaders, or those with higher social status while neglecting those who are struggling financially.

Proverbs 22:2 – "Rich and poor have this in common: The Lord is the Maker of them all."

- **Cultural or Racial Divisions:** Many churches unintentionally create divisions based on ethnicity, background, or traditions, making certain groups feel unwelcome.

Revelation 7:9 – "After this I looked, and there before me was a great multitude that no one could count, from every nation, tribe, people and language, standing before the throne and before the Lamb."

- **Favoritism in Ministry Opportunities:** Leadership roles or ministry positions may be given to certain individuals based on personal relationships rather than spiritual calling and character.

1st Samuel 16:7 – "But the Lord said to Samuel, 'Do not consider his appearance or his height, for I have rejected him. The Lord does not look at the things people look at. People look at the outward appearance, but the Lord looks at the heart.'"

- **Neglecting the Marginalized:** The poor, homeless, disabled, or those with difficult pasts (such as former addicts or ex-prisoners) may be overlooked or treated as less important.

Luke 14:13–14 – "But when you give a banquet, invite the poor, the crippled, the lame, the blind, and you will be blessed. Although they cannot repay you, you will be repaid at the resurrection of the righteous."

How can we guard against favoritism in the church?

- **Recognizing Everyone's Equal Value in Christ:** We must regularly remind ourselves and others that every person is created in God's image and has equal worth in His eyes.

James 2:1 – "My brothers and sisters, believers in our glorious Lord Jesus Christ must not show favoritism."

- **Intentionally Welcoming and Including All People:** Make a conscious effort to greet and include people from all backgrounds in church activities, ministries, and fellowship.

Romans 12:16 – "Live in harmony with one another. Do not be proud, but be willing to associate with people of low position. Do not be conceited."

- **Serving with Impartiality:** Church leadership should strive to give equal opportunities for service and ministry based on spiritual gifting rather than external factors.

Colossians 3:23–24 – "Whatever you do, work at it with all your heart, as working for the Lord, not for human masters, since you know that you will receive an inheritance from the Lord as a reward. It is the Lord Christ you are serving."

- **Examining Our Hearts and Biases:** Each believer should regularly pray for God to reveal personal prejudices and ask for His help in overcoming them.

Psalm 139:23–24 – "Search me, God, and know my heart; test me and know my anxious thoughts. See if there is any offensive way in me, and lead me in the way everlasting."

- **Teaching and Modeling Biblical Love:** Leaders should preach and model a Christlike love that includes everyone, regardless of background, wealth, or social standing.

John 13:34–35 (NIV) – "A new command I give you: Love one another. As I have loved you, so you must love one another. By this everyone will know that you are my disciples if you love one another."

How does favoritism contradict the heart of the Gospel?

- **Equality in Christ:** The Gospel teaches that all are equal before God, so showing favoritism undermines the inclusive love of Christ.

Galatians 3:28 – "There is neither Jew nor Gentile, neither slave nor free, nor is there male and female, for you are all one in Christ Jesus."

Romans 2:11 – "For God does not show favoritism."

- **Distorted Justice:** Showing partiality results in unfair treatment and division, contrary to God's call to love our neighbor as ourselves.

Leviticus 19:15 – "Do not pervert justice; do not show partiality to the poor or favoritism to the great, but judge your neighbor fairly."

Proverbs 22:2 – "Rich and poor have this in common: The Lord is the Maker of them all."

- **Call to Impartiality:** True faith reflects God's impartial nature, where every person is valued regardless of their status or wealth.

Acts 10:34–35 – "Then Peter began to speak: 'I now realize how true it is that God does not show favoritism but accepts from every nation the one who fears him and does what is right.'"

Colossians 3:11 – "Here there is no Gentile or Jew, circumcised or uncircumcised, barbarian, Scythian, slave or free, but Christ is all, and is in all."

James 2:8–13 – "If you really keep the royal law…"

How does loving our neighbor fulfill the law, and what does that look like practically?

- **Love in Action:** Loving our neighbor means actively caring for others—meeting needs, showing compassion, and practicing forgiveness.

1ˢᵗ John 4:7 – "Dear friends, let us love one another, for love comes from God. Everyone who loves has been born of God and knows God."

Matthew 25:40 – "The King will reply, 'Truly I tell you, whatever you did for one of the least of these brothers and sisters of mine, you did for me.'"

- **Fulfilling the Law:** It's a practical demonstration of the law's intent; by loving others, we uphold God's command to treat one another with dignity and respect.

Romans 13:8–10 – "Let no debt remain outstanding, except the continuing debt to love one another, for whoever loves others has fulfilled the law. The commandments… are summed up in this one command: 'Love your neighbor as yourself.' Love does no harm to a neighbor. Therefore, love is the fulfillment of the law."

John 13:34–35 – "A new command I give you: Love one another. As I have loved you, so you must love one another. By this everyone will know that you are my disciples, if you love one another."

- **Community Building:** Practically, this can involve reaching out to the marginalized, advocating for justice, and creating inclusive environments.

Micah 6:8 – "He has shown you, O mortal, what is good. And what does the Lord require of you? To act justly and to love mercy and to walk humbly with your God."

Hebrews 10:24 – "And let us consider how we may spur one another on toward love and good deeds."

Session 4 - Key Summary Points

1. **James 2:1–7 – "My brothers and sisters, believers in our glorious Lord…"**

- Faith in Christ should not include favoritism—all people have equal worth before God.
- Showing special treatment to the wealthy while dishonoring the poor is inconsistent with God's values.
- God often chooses the poor in the world to be rich in faith, while the rich can sometimes exploit others.
- True faith honors people based on God's love, not social status.

2. **James 2:8–13 – "If you really keep the royal law found in Scripture…"**

- The "royal law" is to love your neighbor as yourself (Leviticus 19:18).
- Favoritism is a sin and makes a person guilty of breaking God's law.
- God's law is unified—breaking one part makes someone a lawbreaker.
- Mercy triumphs over judgment—believers should extend mercy as they will be judged by the standard they use.

A. Favoritism Contradicts the Gospel

When we show partiality—whether by status, appearance, influence, or background—we go against the very heart of the gospel. God doesn't choose people based on merit; He loves all equally. We are called to love with that same heart.

Cross-reference: Romans 2:11 – "For God does not show favoritism."

B. Everyone Has Equal Worth in God's Eyes

We may not realize it, but subtle behaviors (like avoiding certain people or valuing others more) can communicate exclusion. God sees the unseen, honors the lowly, and calls us to treat everyone with dignity and compassion.

Cross-reference: 1 Samuel 16:7 – "People look at the outward appearance, but the Lord looks at the heart."

C. Mercy Reflects the Heart of God

James says, "mercy triumphs over judgment" (v.13). When we extend kindness to those overlooked, we reflect the very nature of Christ, who sought out the marginalized and forgotten.

Cross-reference: Micah 6:8 – "To act justly and to love mercy and to walk humbly with your God."

D. Jesus Modeled Radical Inclusion

From tax collectors to lepers, Jesus constantly reached out to those society avoided. Our faith in Him should lead us to ask: Who am I overlooking? Who needs love, inclusion, or encouragement?

Cross-reference: Luke 14:13–14 – Jesus urges us to invite the poor, the crippled, the blind, and the lame.

Closing Question:

"How can you be more intentional about treating others with the same love and mercy that God has shown you?"

Challenge:

- Look around your workplace, your church, or your social group—who might feel unseen or excluded?
- What's one simple way you can extend God's love and attention to someone who usually doesn't get it?

Struggle: Overcoming favoritism.

Practical Steps:

- Intentionally befriend people outside your usual social circle.
- Serve in outreach programs for marginalized communities.
- Pray for a heart that reflects God's impartial love.

Conclusion:

James challenges us to examine our hearts when it comes to how we treat others. *Do we show favoritism? Do we value people based on status, appearance, or what they can do for us?* The heart of the Gospel is that God shows no partiality, and we are called to love others as He loves us.

True faith does not elevate the rich and powerful while neglecting the poor and humble. Instead, it sees every person as valuable in the eyes of God. The law of love—the royal law—calls us to love our neighbor as ourselves, showing mercy rather than judgment.

Key Reflection:

Are there areas in our lives where we show favoritism? Do we truly extend grace, love, and honor to everyone, regardless of their background? Let's ask God to help us reflect His mercy in the way we treat others, knowing that mercy triumphs over judgment.

Closing Prayer:

Gracious God, thank You for showing no favoritism. Forgive us when we make judgments based on outward appearances. Teach us to love as You love—with mercy, compassion, and equity. Help us to reflect Christ's love in all our relationships, especially to those who are often overlooked. In Jesus' name, we pray, Amen.

Session 5

James 2:14–26 – Do you have "faith with works" or "faith without works?"

Faith without works is dead—this simple yet profound statement from James challenges us to evaluate the authenticity of our faith. In this session, we will learn that true faith manifests itself in actions that align with God's will. As we examine the examples of Abraham and Rahab, we will reflect on how our faith can be made complete through works. Let us consider how our actions speak louder than words in demonstrating the reality of our beliefs.

Session 5: James 2:14–26

- James 2:14–17: "What good is it, my brothers and sisters…"
- James 2:18–26: "Faith by itself, if it is not accompanied by action…"

14 What good is it, my brothers and sisters, if someone claims to have faith but has no deeds? Can such faith save them? **15** Suppose a brother or a sister is without clothes and daily food. **16** If one of you says to them, "Go in peace; keep warm and well fed," but does nothing about their physical needs, what good is it? **17** In the same way, faith by itself, if it is not accompanied by action, is dead. **18** But someone will say, "You have faith; I have deeds." Show me your faith without deeds, and I will show you my faith by my deeds. **19** You believe that there is one God. Good! Even the demons believe that—and shudder. **20** You foolish person, do you want evidence that faith without deeds is useless? **21** Was not our father Abraham considered righteous for what he did when he offered his son Isaac on the altar? **22** You see that his faith and his actions were working together, and his faith was made complete by what he did. **23** And the scripture was fulfilled that says, "Abraham believed God, and it was credited to him as righteousness," and he was called God's friend. **24** You see that a person is considered righteous by what they do and not by faith alone. **25** In the same way, was not even Rahab the prostitute considered righteous for what she did when she gave lodging to the spies and sent them off in a different direction? **26** As the body without the spirit is dead, so faith without deeds is dead.

James 2:14–17 – "What good is it, my brothers and sisters…"

Why must faith be accompanied by action?

- **Proof of Genuine Faith:** Faith without works is lifeless; true faith is demonstrated through action.

Matthew 7:16-17 – "By their fruit you will recognize them. Do people pick grapes from thornbushes, or figs from thistles? Likewise, every good tree bears good fruit, but a bad tree bears bad fruit."

- **Living Testimony:** Our actions testify to the reality of our faith, showing the love of Christ to the world.

Titus 3:8 – "This is a trustworthy saying. And I want you to stress these things, so that those who have trusted in God may be careful to devote themselves to doing what is good. These things are excellent and profitable for everyone."

- **Faith and Works Complement Each Other:** Works do not replace faith but are the natural outflow of it.

Ephesians 2:10 – "For we are God's handiwork, created in Christ Jesus to do good works, which God prepared in advance for us to do."

Can Faith Exist Without Works? Why or Why Not?

- **Faith Without Works Is Dead:** The Bible clearly teaches that faith without works is lifeless and ineffective. True faith naturally produces good deeds.

James 2:26 – "As the body without the spirit is dead, so faith without deeds is dead."

- **Works Are the Evidence of Genuine Faith:** While salvation is by grace through faith alone, works serve as the visible proof of an inward transformation.

Matthew 7:21 – "Not everyone who says to me, 'Lord, Lord,' will enter the kingdom of heaven, but only the one who does the will of my Father who is in heaven."

- **Faith and Works Are Inseparable:** Works do not earn salvation, but they naturally flow from a heart that has been changed by Christ.

Ephesians 2:8-10 – "For it is by grace you have been saved, through faith—and this is not from yourselves, it is the gift of God—not by works, so that no one can boast. For we are God's handiwork, created in Christ Jesus to do good works, which God prepared in advance for us to do."

James 2:18–26 – "Faith by itself, if it is not accompanied by action..."

What are some tangible ways we can demonstrate our faith through action?

- **Service to Others:** Showing kindness and generosity through acts of service.

Galatians 5:13 – "You, my brothers and sisters, were called to be free. But do not use your freedom to indulge the flesh; rather, serve one another humbly in love."

- **Consistent Obedience:** Living out biblical principles in daily life—honesty, integrity, and love.

John 14:15 – "If you love me, keep my commands."

1. **Community Impact**: Engaging in outreach, helping the poor, and being a light to the world.

Matthew 5:16 – "Let your light shine before others, that they may see your good deeds and glorify your Father in heaven."

Session 5 - Key Summary Points

1. **James 2:14–17 – "What good is it, my brothers and sisters..."**

- **Faith without works is dead**—genuine faith is not just a profession but is demonstrated through actions.
- Saying you have faith is meaningless if it doesn't **lead to love and action** towards others, especially those in need.
- **True faith** moves a believer to help others and make a tangible difference in their lives.

2. **James 2:18–26 – "Faith by itself, if it is not accompanied by action…"**

- Faith is **validated by deeds**, not merely words or beliefs.
- **Abraham's faith** was demonstrated when he offered Isaac, showing that faith and works go hand in hand.
- **Rahab's actions** (hiding the spies) proved her faith, further illustrating that faith must be active.
- Just as the **body without the spirit is dead**, faith without works is also dead—faith must be living and active to be true.

A. Genuine Faith Produces Action

True faith is more than belief—it's trust that results in obedience. Just like a tree naturally bears fruit, living faith shows itself in acts of love, service, and obedience to God.

Cross-reference: Matthew 7:17 – "Every good tree bears good fruit."

B. Faith and Works Are Two Sides of the Same Coin

James isn't saying we earn salvation through works but that faith and action are inseparable. A heart changed by Christ will lead to a life that reflects His character.

Cross-reference: Ephesians 2:8–10 – "For it is by grace you have been saved… created in Christ Jesus to do good works."

C. Examples of Faith in Action

Abraham trusted God so deeply he was willing to sacrifice Isaac—his actions proved his faith. Rahab risked her life to protect the

Israelite spies because she believed in the power of their God. Their stories remind us that faith shows up in big and small choices alike.

Cross-reference: Hebrews 11:8 & 31 – Faith led both Abraham and Rahab to act courageously.

D. Living Faith Meets Real Needs

James 2:15–16 challenges us not just to say kind words but to respond to real needs. Faith reaches out—feeding the hungry, helping the lonely, and serving others as Christ would.

Cross-reference: 1 John 3:17–18 – "Let us not love with words or speech but with actions and in truth."

Closing Question:

"How can you make sure that your faith is not just a belief but something that drives you to action in your daily life?

Challenge

- Ask yourself: If someone looked at my life this week, what would they see my faith in?
- Identify one act of service or compassion you can offer this week that expresses your trust in and love for Christ.

Struggle: Putting faith into action.

Practical Steps:

- Look for ways to serve others regularly.
- Support missions or charitable organizations.
- Take small faith-driven risks to grow spiritually.

Conclusion:

James challenges us to examine whether our faith is truly alive. A genuine faith is not just about belief—it is evidenced by action. Faith and works are not opposing forces; rather, they work together. Just as the body without the spirit is dead, faith without works is lifeless.

Abraham's willingness to sacrifice Isaac and Rahab's courageous protection of the spies show that obedience to God flows from faith. If our faith is real, it will naturally lead us to love, serve, and act in obedience.

Key Reflection:

Does our faith move us to action? This week, let's look for opportunities to live out our faith—whether through acts of kindness, generosity, or obedience to God's leading. Faith must be visible to be alive.

Closing Prayer:

Lord, may our faith be alive and active. Teach us that faith is not just belief but obedience in action. Give us hearts willing to serve, hands ready to help, and lives that testify of Your grace. Help us to live in such a way that others see our good works and glorify You. In Jesus' name, Amen.

Session 6

James 3:1–12 – How does mastery of one's speech keep the whole body in check?

Words have incredible power. They can build up or tear down, heal or hurt. James teaches that the tongue, though small, holds immense power to direct the course of our lives. In this session, we will examine the responsibility we have in controlling our speech and the impact it can have on our relationships and spiritual growth. Let us ask the Holy Spirit to guide our words so that they reflect God's love and truth.

Session 6: James 3:1–12

- James 3:1–6: "Not many of you should become teachers…"
- James 3:7–12: "All kinds of animals, birds, reptiles and fish…"

1 Not many of you should become teachers, my fellow believers because you know that we who teach will be judged more strictly. **2** We all stumble in many ways. Anyone who is never at fault in what they say is perfect, able to keep their whole body in check. **3** When we put bits into the mouths of horses to make them obey us, we can turn the whole animal. **4** Or take ships as an example. Although they are so large and are driven by strong winds, they are steered by a very small rudder wherever the pilot wants to go. **5** Likewise, the tongue is a small part of the body, but it makes great boasts. Consider what a great forest is set on fire by a small spark. **6** The tongue also is a fire, a world of evil among the parts of the body. It corrupts the whole body, sets the whole course of one's life on fire, and is itself set on fire by hell. **7** All kinds of animals, birds, reptiles and sea creatures are being tamed and have been tamed by mankind, **8** but no human being can tame the tongue. It is a restless evil, full of deadly poison. **9** With the tongue, we praise our Lord and Father, and with it, we curse human beings who have been made in God's likeness. **10** Out of the same mouth come praise and cursing. My brothers and sisters, this should not be. **11** Can both fresh water and salt water flow from the same spring? **12** My brothers and sisters, can a fig tree bear olives or a grapevine bear figs? Neither can a salt spring produce fresh water.

James 3:1–6 – "Not many of you should become teachers..."

How can our words impact our faith and relationships?

- **Powerful Influence:** Words have the power to build or destroy. They reflect the state of our hearts and can deeply impact others, influencing their faith and relationships with God and others.

Proverbs 18:21 – "The tongue has the power of life and death, and those who love it will eat its fruit."

Matthew 12:34-37 – "For the mouth speaks what the heart is full of. A good man brings good things out of the good stored up in him, and an evil man brings evil things out of the evil stored up in him. But I tell you that everyone will have to give account on the day of judgment for every empty word they have spoken."

- **Reflecting God's Nature:** Our words are a reflection of God's nature in us. When we speak with kindness, encouragement, and truth, we imitate the character of Christ.

Ephesians 4:29 – "Do not let any unwholesome talk come out of your mouths, but only what is helpful for building others up according to their needs, that it may benefit those who listen."

Colossians 4:6 – "Let your conversation be always full of grace, seasoned with salt, so that you may know how to answer everyone."

- **Guarding Against Harm:** By carefully controlling our speech, we can avoid causing unnecessary harm and prevent misunderstandings. Thoughtful speech fosters healthier relationships and aligns with God's peace.

Proverbs 15:1 – "A gentle answer turns away wrath, but a harsh word stirs up anger."

James 1:19 – "My dear brothers and sisters, take note of this: Everyone should be quick to listen, slow to speak and slow to become angry."

James 3:7–12 – "All kinds of animals... but no human being can tame the tongue..."

In what ways can we use our words to bring life and encouragement instead of harm?

- **Speaking Life:** Words should be a source of encouragement and life, reinforcing the dignity of others and pointing them toward God's truth and love.

Proverbs 16:24 – "Gracious words are a honeycomb, sweet to the soul and healing to the bones."

1st Thessalonians 5:11 – "Therefore encourage one another and build each other up, just as in fact you are doing."

- **Intentional Communication:** Being intentional about our words means taking a moment to consider their impact before speaking, ensuring our words are positive and constructive.

Proverbs 21:23 – "Those who guard their mouths and their tongues keep themselves from calamity."

Ephesians 4:29 – "Do not let any unwholesome talk come out of your mouths, but only what is helpful for building others up according to their needs, that it may benefit those who listen."

- **Modeling Christ's Example:** Jesus is the perfect example of how to use words to bring healing, truth, and love. By following His example, we can use our speech to reflect His character.

1st Peter 3:9 – "Do not repay evil with evil or insult with insult. On the contrary, repay evil with blessing, because to this you were called so that you may inherit a blessing."

Matthew 12:34-37 – "For the mouth speaks what the heart is full of... By your words you will be acquitted, and by your words you will be condemned."

Session 6 - Key Summary Points

1. **James 3:1–6 – "Not many of you should become teachers..."**

- Teaching comes with great responsibility, as teachers will be judged more strictly.

- The tongue is a powerful tool that can either build up or destroy, and we must be careful with our words.
- Just as a small bit controls a horse or a small rudder steers a ship, the tongue, though small, has great power to direct our lives.
- Uncontrolled speech can cause great harm, like a spark starting a fire, and can lead to destruction.

2. **James 3:7–12 – "All kinds of animals, birds, reptiles and fish…"**

- Humans can tame animals, but the tongue is difficult to tame and is often filled with both blessing and cursing.
- It is inconsistent and hypocritical to bless God with our tongues and curse others who are made in God's image.
- The tongue should not produce both good and evil—praise and curse cannot come from the same mouth.
- James challenges believers to recognize that true wisdom is reflected in a consistent, loving, and controlled use of the tongue.

A. Words Have Power—Choose Them Wisely

James compares the tongue to a bit in a horse's mouth or a rudder on a ship—small but powerful. Our words have the power to steer our lives and influence others—either toward healing or harm.

Cross-reference: Proverbs 18:21 – "The tongue has the power of life and death…"

B. The Tongue Reflects the Heart

What comes out of our mouths reveals what's going on inside our minds and hearts. If our speech is often angry, gossipy, or ungrateful, it's time to ask God to renew our hearts.

Cross-reference: Luke 6:45 – "Out of the abundance of the heart the mouth speaks."

C. Surrender Speech to the Spirit

We cannot tame the tongue on our own—James says that clearly and explicitly. But with the help of the Holy Spirit, we can speak words that are seasoned with grace and truth.

Cross-reference: Ephesians 4:29 – "Do not let any unwholesome talk come out of your mouths, but only what is helpful for building others up..."

D. Speak with Intentional Kindness and Truth

Using our words to glorify God doesn't mean being fake—it means being intentional. Speak life. Speak encouragement. Speak the truth in love. Speak peace into conflict. These things reflect God's nature.

Cross-reference: Colossians 4:6 – "Let your conversation be always full of grace, seasoned with salt..."

E. Avoid Hypocrisy in Speech

James reminds us it's inconsistent and downright wrong to praise God on Sunday and engage in gossip on Monday. We glorify God when we align what we say with who He is—integrity matters.

Cross-reference: Psalm 19:14 – "May the words of my mouth and the meditation of my heart be pleasing in your sight, O Lord..."

Closing Question:

"How can you become more mindful of the power of your words and ensure that they reflect God's love and wisdom?"

Challenge

- This week, ask God to put a guard over your mouth (Psalm 141:3).
- Before you speak, pause and ask, "Will this glorify God or just gratify myself?"
- Consider how you can use words to encourage someone this week—maybe through a message, a conversation, or a prayer.

Struggle: Controlling the tongue.

Practical Steps:

- Pause before speaking and ask if your words are helpful, fulfilling, uplifting, or hurtful.
- Replace negative speech with praise and encouragement.
- Confess and repent when speaking carelessly.

Conclusion:

James reminds us of the incredible power of our words—they can build up or tear down, bless or curse. The tongue is small but mighty, capable of setting lives on fire for good or evil. As followers of Christ, we must surrender to and align our speech with God and seek to reflect His truth, grace, and wisdom in how we communicate and hold conversations.

Words are an outflow of the heart. If our words are consistently unkind, deceitful, or negative, we must examine what's taking root inside us. Instead of allowing the tongue to be a destructive force, we can yield it to God and use it to bring life and encouragement to others.

Key Reflection:

Are our words reflecting Christ or causing harm? This week, let's make a conscious effort to speak life, encouragement, and truth, using our words as instruments of God's love and wisdom.

Closing Prayer:

Father, we surrender our speech to You. Help us to use our words to build up and not tear down. Forgive us for the careless things we've said. Forgive us for what we said when we were overtaken by emotion. Fill our mouths with truth, kindness, and encouragement. May our speech be seasoned with grace and bring glory to Your name. In Christ, Amen.

Session 7

James 3:13–18 – What is wisdom?
What is not wisdom?

There are two types of wisdom: godly wisdom and worldly wisdom. One leads to peace, righteousness, and humility, while the other fosters jealousy, selfish ambition, and disorder. In this session, we will explore how to distinguish between the two and how godly wisdom can guide our decisions, relationships, and actions. Let us open our hearts to seek wisdom that comes from above, which is pure, peace-loving, and full of mercy.

Session 7: James 3:13–18

- James 3:13–16: "Who is wise and understanding among you?"
- James 3:17–18: "But the wisdom that comes from heaven is first…"

13 Who is wise and understanding among you? Let them show it by their good life, by deeds done in the humility that comes from wisdom. 14 But if you harbor bitter envy and selfish ambition in your hearts, do not boast about it or deny the truth. 15 Such "wisdom" does not come down from heaven but is earthly, unspiritual, demonic. 16 For where you have envy and selfish ambition, there you find disorder and every evil practice. 17 But the wisdom that comes from heaven is first of all pure; then peace-loving, considerate, submissive, full of mercy and good fruit,

impartial and sincere. **18** Peacemakers who sow in peace reap a harvest of righteousness.

James 3:13–16 – "Who is wise and understanding among you?"

How can we recognize godly wisdom versus worldly wisdom?

- **Characteristics of Godly Wisdom:** Godly wisdom is marked by **purity**, **humility**, and a **desire for peace**. It focuses on serving others and bringing about and establishing lasting harmony rather than seeking personal gain or recognition.

Proverbs 2:6 – "For the Lord gives wisdom; from his mouth come knowledge and understanding."

James 3:17 – "But the wisdom that comes from heaven is first of all pure; then peace-loving, considerate, submissive, full of mercy and good fruit, impartial and sincere."

Philippians 2:3-4 – "Do nothing out of selfish ambition or vain conceit. Rather, in humility value others above yourselves, not looking to your own interests but each of you to the interests of the others."

- **Contrast with Worldly Wisdom:** Worldly wisdom is often focused on **self-promotion**, **power**, and the pursuit of **immediate gain**. It can lead to conflict, division, and strife, reflecting the values of the world rather than the values of God's kingdom.

1st Corinthians 3:19 – "For the wisdom of this world is foolishness in God's sight. As it is written: 'He catches the wise in their craftiness.'"

Proverbs 14:12 – "There is a way that appears to be right, but in the end it leads to death."

- **Living Out Wisdom:** Evaluate your **decisions** and **actions** against **biblical principles**. Godly wisdom always leads to outcomes that honor God, promote peace, and build up others, as opposed to promoting selfish ambition or conflict.

Colossians 3:16 – "Let the message of Christ dwell among you richly as you teach and admonish one another with all wisdom through psalms, hymns, and songs from the Spirit, singing to God with gratitude in your hearts."

Proverbs 3:5-6 – "Trust in the Lord with all your heart and lean not on your own understanding; in all your ways submit to him, and he will make your paths straight."

James 3:17–18 – "But the wisdom that comes from heaven is first…"

What are the practical effects of embracing wisdom from above?

- **Fruits of Peace: Heavenly wisdom** brings about **inner peace, self-control**, and **kindness**. These qualities naturally pave the way for harmonious relationships to blossom and prosper and contribute to peaceful environments.

Isaiah 32:17 – "The fruit of that righteousness will be peace; its effect will be quietness and confidence forever."

Romans 14:19 – "Let us therefore make every effort to do what leads to peace and to mutual edification."

- **Positive Influence:** Embracing godly wisdom produces good **fruit** in our lives, leading to **mercy**, **patience**, and genuine care for others. It inspires actions that demonstrate God's love and compassion.

Galatians 5:22-23 – "But the fruit of the Spirit is love, joy, peace, forbearance, kindness, goodness, faithfulness, gentleness and self-control. Against such things, there is no law."

Matthew 5:9 – "Blessed are the peacemakers, for they will be called children of God."

- **Long-Term Benefits:** Embracing godly wisdom helps us navigate life's challenges with **clarity**, **purpose**, and **God's guidance**, leading us to make decisions that align with His will. This wisdom equips and fortifies us to handle difficulties with faith and trust in God's sovereignty.

Proverbs 4:7 – "The beginning of wisdom is this: Get wisdom. Though it cost all you have, get understanding."

James 1:5 – "If any of you lacks wisdom, let him ask of God, who gives generously to all without finding fault, and it will be given to him."

Session 7 - Key Summary Points

1. **James 3:13–16 – "Who is wise and understanding among you?"**

- True wisdom is demonstrated through humility and good deeds, not boasting or pride.

- Earthly wisdom, rooted in selfishness and envy, leads to disorder and conflict.
- Selfish ambition and bitter envy destroy peace, making a person's wisdom unwise and divisive.
- True wisdom is not about outward appearance or knowledge but about living out godly principles with a humble and peace-loving heart.

2. **James 3:17–18 – "But the wisdom that comes from heaven is first..."**

- Heavenly wisdom is pure, peace-loving, considerate, submissive, full of mercy, good fruit, impartial, and sincere.
- It leads to peace and righteousness—sowing seeds of peace that bear good fruit in our lives and relationships.
- God's wisdom is not just about knowing what is right but also acting on it with love and integrity, promoting harmony and righteousness.

A. Godly Wisdom Flows from a Humble Heart

James begins with a challenge: "Who is wise and understanding among you? Let them show it by their good life..." True wisdom isn't loud or self-promoting—it's humble, submitted, and lived out in actions.

Cross-reference: Proverbs 11:2 – "When pride comes, then comes disgrace, but with humility comes wisdom."

B. Worldly Wisdom Promotes Self—Godly Wisdom Promotes Peace

Worldly wisdom often comes cloaked in cleverness, ambition, or even manipulation. But godly wisdom seeks peace, unity, and righteousness—not just personal gain.

Cross-reference: 1 Corinthians 3:19 – "For the wisdom of this world is foolishness in God's sight…"

C. Godly Wisdom Bears Good Fruit

James gives a beautiful list in verse 17: purity, peace-loving, considerate, submissive, full of mercy, good fruit, impartial, and sincere. These are signs of a life being shaped by heaven, not just by knowledge.

Cross-reference: Matthew 7:16 – "By their fruit you will recognize them."

D. Discernment Is a Gift, Not a Given

God invites us to ask for wisdom, reminding us it's not automatic—we must seek it intentionally, especially when making decisions.

Cross-reference: Proverbs 3:5–7 – "Trust in the Lord… do not lean on your own understanding…"

E. Wisdom Impacts Community

James ends by saying, "Peacemakers who sow in peace reap a harvest of righteousness." Wise people build communities, not cliques. They foster healing, not division.

Cross-reference: Romans 12:18 – "If it is possible… live at peace with everyone."

Closing Question:

"How can you actively seek and apply heavenly wisdom in your relationships and daily decisions to promote peace and righteousness?

Challenge

- When making a decision this week, ask: "Am I being led by selfish ambition or spiritual peace?"
- Choose one of the traits in James 3:17 and intentionally practice it—perhaps being gentle or open to reason.
- Begin praying regularly, "Lord, help me walk in Your wisdom, not just my opinion."

Struggle: Seeking godly wisdom over worldly wisdom.

Practical Steps:

- Pray for discernment before making decisions.
- Study Proverbs and James to understand godly wisdom.
- Surround yourself with wise, godly people and seek counsel from God-loving mentors.

Conclusion:

James presents two contrasting kinds of wisdom: earthly wisdom, which is rooted in envy, selfish ambition, and disorder, and heavenly wisdom, which is pure, peace-loving, and full of mercy. The wisdom we choose to follow will shape our relationships, decisions, and, ultimately, our character.

True wisdom is not found in arrogance or personal gain but in humility and submission to God. When we seek His wisdom, it produces peace, righteousness, and godly fruit in our lives. The world promotes self-centered wisdom, but God calls us to wisdom that seeks His will above all.

Key Reflection:

What kind of wisdom are we pursuing? Let's commit to seeking God's wisdom daily through prayer, His Word, and a humble heart, allowing it to shape our thoughts, words, and actions.

Closing Prayer:

God of wisdom, thank You for showing us the difference between worldly thinking and Your truth. Fill us with the wisdom that is pure, peace-loving, considerate, and full of mercy. Guide our decisions and shape our character. Help us sow peace in a world that so often breeds division.

In Jesus' name, Amen.

Session 8

James 4:1–12 – Are you asking God what He wants for you?

Conflicts often arise when we pursue our own desires without considering God's will. James reminds us that submission to God's will brings peace and resolves conflicts in our hearts and lives. This session invites us to examine the sources of our quarrels and desires and encourages us to align our hearts with God's desires. Let's reflect on the importance of resisting pride and submitting ourselves to the one true source of peace.

Session 8: James 4:1–12

- James 4:1–3: "What causes fights and quarrels among you?"
- James 4:4–6: "You adulterous people, don't you know…"
- James 4:7–12: "Submit yourselves, then, to God…"

1 What causes fights and quarrels among you? Don't they come from your desires that battle within you? 2 You desire but do not have, so you kill. You covet but you cannot get what you want, so you quarrel and fight. You do not have because you do not ask God. 3 When you ask, you do not receive, because you ask with wrong motives, that you may spend what you get on your pleasures. 4 You adulterous people, don't you know that friendship with the world means enmity against God? Therefore, anyone who chooses to be a friend of the world becomes an enemy of God. 5 Or do you think Scripture says without reason that he jealously longs for the spirit he has caused to dwell in us? 6 But he gives us more grace. That is why

Scripture says: "God opposes the proud but shows favor to the humble." **7** Submit yourselves, then, to God. Resist the devil, and he will flee from you. **8** Come near to God and he will come near to you. Wash your hands, you sinners, and purify your hearts, you double-minded. **9** Grieve, mourn and wail. Change your laughter to mourning and your joy to gloom. **10** Humble yourselves before the Lord, and he will lift you up. **11** Brothers and sisters, do not slander one another. Anyone who speaks against a brother or sister or judges them speaks against the law and judges it. When you judge the law, you are not keeping it, but sitting in judgment on it. **12** There is only one Lawgiver and Judge, the one who is able to save and destroy. But you—who are you to judge your neighbor?

James 4:1–3 – "What causes fights and quarrels among you?"

How do selfish desires lead to conflict, and how can we surrender them to God?

- **Source of Conflict:** Selfish desires often create division, envy, and competition, leading to quarrels and discord in relationships and interactions. These desires come from our own hearts, driven by a longing for self-centered fulfillment.

Galatians 5:19-21 – *"The acts of the flesh are obvious: sexual immorality, impurity and debauchery; idolatry and witchcraft; hatred, discord, jealousy, fits of rage, selfish ambition, dissensions, factions and envy... I warn you, as I did before, that those who live like this will not inherit the kingdom of God."*

Proverbs 13:10 – *"Where there is strife, there is pride, but wisdom is found in those who take advice."*

- **Need for Surrender:** Recognizing that these selfish desires come from within helps us consciously surrender them to

God, allowing His will to replace our own. This process brings peace and restores relationships.

Philippians 4:6-7 – "Do not be anxious about anything, but in every situation, by prayer and petition, with thanksgiving, present your requests to God. And the peace of God, which transcends all understanding, will guard your hearts and your minds in Christ Jesus."

Matthew 11:29-30 – "Take my yoke upon you and learn from me, for I am gentle and humble in heart, and you will find rest for your souls. For my yoke is easy and my burden is light."

- **Path to Unity**: By submitting our desires to God, we invite His peace into our relationships. This act of surrender fosters unity and understanding among people, bringing the body of Christ together.

Ephesians 4:3 – "Make every effort to keep the unity of the Spirit through the bond of peace."

Romans 12:18 – "If it is possible, as far as it depends on you, live at peace with everyone."

James 4:4–6 – "You adulterous people, don't you know…"

What does it mean to be a friend of the world versus a friend of God?

- **Conflicting Loyalties:** Being a friend of the world means prioritizing worldly values over God's. This leads to compromised priorities and divided loyalties, causing spiritual conflict and disconnect from God's will.

71

Matthew 6:24 – "No one can serve two masters. Either you will hate the one and love the other, or you will be devoted to the one and despise the other."

1st John 2:15-17 – "Do not love the world or anything in the world. If anyone loves the world, love for the Father is not in them. For everything in the world—the lust of the flesh, the lust of the eyes, and the pride of life—comes not from the Father but from the world."

- **True Friendship with God:** True friendship with God requires rejecting the fleeting pleasures of the world and aligning our lives with eternal truths. This means living out God's values and priorities, which last beyond the temporary things of the world.

John 15:14-15 – "You are my friends if you do what I command. I no longer call you servants, because a servant does not know his master's business. Instead, I have called you friends, for everything that I learned from my Father I have made known to you."

Romans 12:2 – "Do not conform to the pattern of this world, but be transformed by the renewing of your mind. Then you will be able to test and approve what God's will is—his good, pleasing, and perfect will."

- **Heart Transformation:** A genuine relationship with God transforms our **priorities** and enables us to live out His principles, as we are made more like Christ. This transformation affects every aspect of our lives—cleansing us and renewing us from within.

2nd Corinthians 5:17 – "Therefore, if anyone is in Christ, the new creation has come: The old has gone, the new is here!"

Romans 8:5-6 – "Those who live according to the flesh have their minds set on what the flesh desires; but those who live in accordance with the Spirit have their minds set on what the Spirit desires. The mind governed by the flesh is death, but the mind governed by the Spirit is life and peace."

James 4:7–12 – "Submit yourselves, then, to God…"

What does true submission to God look like in everyday life?

- **Obedient Living**: True submission involves regularly choosing God's will over our own, even when it requires sacrifice. It means obeying God in both the big and small moments of life, even if it means rejecting or abandoning things that we love.

Luke 9:23 – "Then he said to them all: 'Whoever wants to be my disciple must deny themselves and take up their cross daily and follow me.'"

1ˢᵗ Peter 1:14-16 – "As obedient children, do not conform to the evil desires you had when you lived in ignorance. But just as he who called you is holy, so be holy in all you do; for it is written: 'Be holy, because I am holy.'"

- **Active Resistance:** Active resistance involves actively resisting temptations and negative influences in our lives, trusting in God's strength to overcome them.

Ephesians 6:11 – "Put on the full armor of God, so that you can take your stand against the devil's schemes."

1ˢᵗ Peter 5:8-9 – "Be alert and of sober mind. Your enemy, the devil, prowls around like a roaring lion looking for someone to devour. Resist him, standing firm in the faith…"

- **Humility and Trust:** A submissive heart is marked by humility and a deep trust in God's plan for our lives, believing that His way is always best, even when things don't appear to be so or your own mind is telling you otherwise.

James 4:10 – "Humble yourselves before the Lord, and he will lift you up."

Proverbs 3:5-6 – "Trust in the Lord with all your heart and lean not on your own understanding; in all your ways submit to him, and he will make your paths straight."

Session 8 - Key Summary Points

1. **James 4:1–3 – "What causes fights and quarrels among you?"**

- Conflicts arise from selfish desires and coveting what others have.
- People fight because they want things their own way, but their desires go unmet.
- Prayer is essential, but asking with wrong motives (to indulge in selfish desires) will not lead to God's answers.
- True fulfillment comes from aligning our desires with God's will, not seeking selfish gain.

2. **James 4:4–6 – "You adulterous people, don't you know…"**

- Spiritual adultery occurs when we give our loyalty to the world and the devil's ways rather than to God.
- Friendship with the world is hostility toward God, as it draws us away from His purity and holiness.
- God opposes the proud but gives grace to the humble—true humility and submission to God lead to His favor.
- God's grace is greater than our sin, and He desires to help us resist temptation and, consequently, draw closer to Him.

3. **James 4:7–12 – "Submit yourselves, then, to God…"**

- Submission to God is the key to overcoming temptation and resisting the devil.
- Draw near to God, and He will draw near to you—purify your hearts and repent of your sins.
- We are called to humble ourselves before God, acknowledging our need for His grace and help.
- Avoid judgment of others, recognizing that God alone is the ultimate judge.

A. Conflict Often Begins in the Heart

James makes it clear: our quarrels and fights often stem from unmet personal desires, not from external circumstances alone. Take time to ask yourself, "What's really driving my frustration or conflict?"

Cross-reference: Jeremiah 17:9 – "The heart is deceitful above all things…"

B. Selfish Desires Block Powerful Prayers

James 4:3 warns that asking with wrong motives—just to satisfy our own pleasures—leads to unanswered prayers. We grow when we start praying, "Lord, what do *You* want for me?" rather than just, "Here's what *I* want."

Cross-reference: Psalm 37:4 – "Delight yourself in the Lord, and He will give you the desires of your heart."

C. God Is Jealous for You—In a Holy Way

James 4:5–6 speaks of God's jealous longing for our spirit. He doesn't want to share our hearts with the world's values. That jealousy is not possessive—it's protective, born from deep love and intended to bless us with eternal lives.

Cross-reference: Exodus 34:14 – "Do not worship any other god, for the Lord... is a jealous God."

D. Victory Comes Through Submission, Not Striving

"Submit yourselves, then, to God. Resist the devil, and he will flee from you."

Submission isn't weakness, as the world might have you believe—it's choosing to come under God's protection and rule. That's where real strength lives.

Cross-reference: 1 Peter 5:6–9 – "Humble yourselves... resist him, standing firm in the faith."

E. True Humility Builds True Community

Judging others or speaking against them reveals pride, not holiness. James reminds us that God alone is the ultimate and only true judge, and our call is to love and walk humbly.

Cross-reference: Micah 6:8 – "To act justly and to love mercy and to walk humbly with your God."

Closing Question:

"What are some areas in your life where you need to humble yourself and submit more fully to God's will, seeking God's desires over your own—and trusting that He will draw near to you?"

Challenge

- Each morning this week, pray: **"God, what do You want for me today?"** Write down what comes to mind.
- When in conflict, pause and ask, "Is this really about me getting my way?" If so, seek God's better way.
- Choose one practical way to **resist the enemy's influence** (e.g., forgiving someone, confessing envy, turning from comparison).

Struggle: Surrendering desires to God.

Practical Steps:

- Fast and pray for alignment with God's will.
- Daily surrender personal plans in prayer.
- Keep a prayer list to track answered prayers.

Conclusion:

James reveals that selfish desires are the root of conflicts—whether within relationships, the church, or within ourselves. The antidote to pride and quarrels is humble submission to God. When we resist the devil and draw near to God, He draws near to us, transforming our hearts and giving us peace.

True submission is not weakness but strength in surrendering to God's will. It involves trusting Him above our own ambitions and allowing Him to purify our hearts. The call to humility and repentance is a reminder that God lifts up the humble and opposes the proud.

Key Reflection:

Are we humbly submitting to God, or are we still clinging to selfish desires? This week, let's focus on surrendering fully to God, resisting sin, and drawing near to Him in obedience and trust.

Closing Prayer:

Lord, we humble ourselves before You. We confess the times we've followed our own desires instead of seeking Your will. Cleanse our hearts, purify our motives, and teach us to submit fully to You. Help us resist the enemy and walk in Your grace. We long to be near You, Lord. In Jesus' name, Amen.

Session 9

James 4:13–17 – Where does God fit in your plans for your life, your family, your home, your church?

We all make plans, but how often do we consider God's will in those plans? James warns against the presumption of planning without our dependence on God, without recognizing the uncertainty of life. In this session, we will learn to embrace a posture of surrender in all our endeavors, trusting that God knows what is best for us. Let's reflect on how we can submit our future to Him and make Him the center of all our plans.

Session 9: James 4:13–17

- James 4:13–14: "Now listen, you who say…"
- James 4:15–17: "Instead, you ought to say, 'If it is the Lord's will…'"

13 Now listen, you who say, "Today or tomorrow we will go to this or that city, spend a year there, carry on business and make money." **14** Why, you do not even know what will happen tomorrow. What is your life? You are a mist that appears for a little while and then vanishes. **15** Instead, you ought to say, "If it is the Lord's will, we will live and do this or that." **16** As it is, you boast in your arrogant schemes. All such boasting is evil. **17** If anyone, then, knows the good they ought to do and doesn't do it, it is sin for them.

James 4:13–14 – "Now listen, you who say…"

How does acknowledging the uncertainty of life change our approach to planning and decision-making?

- **Dependence on God's Sovereignty:** Recognizing life's uncertainty reminds us that we must rely on **God** rather than our own limited perspective. Understanding that our control is limited encourages us to lean on God for wisdom and guidance in all decisions—which is more lucrative and rewarding.

Proverbs 19:21 – "Many are the plans in a person's heart, but it is the Lord's purpose that prevails."

Psalm 33:10-11 – "The Lord foils the plans of the nations; he thwarts the purposes of the peoples. But the plans of the Lord stand firm forever, the purposes of his heart through all generations."

- **Living with Purpose:** Acknowledging that our plans are subject to God's greater plan encourages us to live intentionally, knowing that each day is a gift from God and that our lives should align with His eternal purposes.

Ephesians 5:15-17 – "Be very careful, then, how you live—not as unwise but as wise, making the most of every opportunity, because the days are evil. Therefore, do not be foolish, but understand what the Lord's will is."

Colossians 3:17 – "And whatever you do, whether in word or deed, do it all in the name of the Lord Jesus, giving thanks to God the Father through him."

- **Flexibility and Trust:** Embracing uncertainty helps us stay flexible and strengthen our trust that God will guide our steps, even when the future is unclear. This mindset allows us to adapt as His will unfolds.

Proverbs 16:9 – "In their hearts humans plan their course, but the Lord establishes their steps."

Isaiah 55:8-9 – "'For my thoughts are not your thoughts, neither are your ways my ways,' declares the Lord. 'As the heavens are higher than the earth, so are my ways higher than your ways and my thoughts than your thoughts.'"

James 4:15–17 – "Instead, you ought to say, 'If it is the Lord's will…'"

How can we better align our plans with God's will?

- **Prayerful Planning:** Begin every decision with prayer, seeking God's guidance. Acknowledge that He knows the end from the beginning, and ask for the courage to accept His will, even when it challenges our own desires.

Philippians 4:6-7 – "Do not be anxious about anything, but in every situation, by prayer and petition, with thanksgiving, present your requests to God. And the peace of God, which transcends all understanding, will guard your hearts and your minds in Christ Jesus."

Jeremiah 29:11 – "'For I know the plans I have for you,' declares the Lord, 'plans to prosper you and not to harm you, plans to give you hope and a future.'"

- **Humility in Decision-Making:** Acknowledge that our plans are limited and God's perspective is perfect. This humility leads us to submit our desires entirely to Him, knowing that He knows what is best for us.

Proverbs 3:5-6 – "Trust in the Lord with all your heart and lean not on your own understanding; in all your ways submit to him, and he will make your paths straight."

Psalm 37:4-5 – "Take delight in the Lord, and he will give you the desires of your heart. Commit your way to the Lord; trust in him and he will do this."

- **Continuous Trust:** Consistently seeking God's will in every aspect of life helps us build a mindset of trust and dependence on His direction. Trusting Him allows us to make decisions that honor His sovereignty and bring us closer to Him and Him to us.

Proverbs 16:3 – "Commit to the Lord whatever you do, and he will establish your plans."

Isaiah 26:3 – "You will keep in perfect peace those whose minds are steadfast, because they trust in you."

Session Nine - Key Summary Points

1. **James 4:13–14 – "Now listen, you who say…"**

- Arrogance in planning: James warns against making plans for the future without considering God's will.
- Life is uncertain, and we cannot control our future; we are like a mist that appears briefly and vanishes.
- We are not guaranteed tomorrow, so we must approach our plans with humility and recognize our dependence on God.

2. **James 4:15–17 – "Instead, you ought to say, 'If it is the Lord's will...'"**

- Humility in speech and action: Acknowledge that God's will should guide our plans, and we should seek His direction in all things.
- Doing the will of God involves more than just words—it requires living out what we know to be right.
- Failing to do what is good when we know it is right is also a form of sin.

A. Acknowledge Life's Fragility and God's Sovereignty

James reminds us that life is "a mist that appears for a little while and then vanishes" (v.14). That doesn't mean our lives are meaningless—it means they are precious and best lived under God's direction.

Cross-reference: Proverbs 27:1 – "Do not boast about tomorrow, for you do not know what a day may bring."

B. Invite God into Every Plan

Saying, "If it is the Lord's will..." (v.15) isn't just a phrase—it's a heart posture of humility. It's not about never making plans; it's about submitting our plans to God's leadership.

Cross-reference: Proverbs 16:9 – "In their hearts humans plan their course, but the Lord establishes their steps."

C. Surrender Is Daily, Not Just Once

Trusting God with our future doesn't happen only at major crossroads. It's choosing to walk with Him today, trusting that He holds tomorrow.

Cross-reference: Matthew 6:34 – "Do not worry about tomorrow... Each day has enough trouble of its own."

D. Obedience in the Present Honors God in the Future

Verse 17 says, "If anyone knows the good they ought to do and doesn't do it, it is sin." That means surrender isn't just passive waiting—it's active obedience to what we know to do today.

Cross-reference: Luke 16:10 – "Whoever can be trusted with very little can also be trusted with much..."

E. God's Plans Are Always Better—Even When We Don't Understand Them Yet

Sometimes, surrender means laying down our idea of success, comfort, or control. But over time, we begin to see that God's ways are higher—*and always good.*

Cross-reference: Isaiah 55:8–9 – "My thoughts are not your thoughts, neither are your ways my ways..."

Closing Question:

"How can you shift your perspective and make your plans with a greater focus on God's will, trusting Him with your future – your friends/family ?"

Challenge

- Write down three major plans or dreams for the future. Next to each one, write: **"If the Lord wills..."** and pray for God's guidance over them.
- Ask: Is there something God has shown me to do today that I've been putting off? Take the first step in obedience.
- Journal how uncertainty has impacted you—then pray, giving those areas of uncertainty over to the Lord with open hands.

Struggle: Including God in future plans.

Practical Steps:

- Make prayer the first step in decision-making.
- Ask God for guidance before setting personal goals.
- Reflect on how God has led in the past.

Conclusion:

James reminds us that life is fleeting—like a mist that appears for a little while and then vanishes. Our plans and ambitions should never be made apart from God's will because He alone holds the future. Instead of boasting about our own plans, we are called to live with humility and dependence on God.

Saying "If the Lord wills" is not just a phrase—it's a posture of the heart. It reflects an awareness that our lives belong to God and that He alone directs our steps. True faith does not merely acknowledge God's sovereignty but actively submits to it.

Key Reflection:

Are we making plans independently, or are we seeking God's guidance? Let's commit to prayerfully include God in every decision, trusting His perfect will over our own ambitions.

Closing Prayer:

Father, we acknowledge that our lives are but a mist. We surrender our plans to You, trusting that Your ways are better and Your timing is perfect. Teach us to live each day with humility, seeking Your will in all things. Guide our steps and be the center of our decisions. In Christ's name, Amen.

Session 10

James 5:1–6 – Where are we storing our treasure? & How can we break free from the idolatry of things and seek first God's kingdom?

Materialism can easily creep into our hearts, blinding us to the true value of the kingdom of God. James warns us against hoarding wealth and exploiting others, calling us instead to live with generosity and a kingdom-first mindset. In this session, we will examine our relationship with money and possessions and consider how we can prioritize God's will over the pursuit of earthly treasure. Let us learn to store up treasures in heaven, where they will never fade.

Session 10: James 5:1–6

- James 5:1–3: "Now listen, you rich people, weep and wail…"
- James 5:4–6: "Look! The wages you failed to pay the workers…"

1 Now listen, you rich people, weep and wail because of the misery that is coming on you. **2** Your wealth has rotted, and moths have eaten your clothes. **3** Your gold and silver are corroded. Their corrosion will testify against you and eat your flesh like fire. You have hoarded wealth in the last days. **4** Look! The wages you failed to pay the workers who mowed your fields are crying out against you. The cries of the harvesters have reached the ears of the Lord Almighty. **5** You have lived on earth in luxury and self-indulgence. You have fattened yourselves in the day of slaughter. **6** You have condemned and murdered the innocent one who was not opposing you.

James 5:1–3 – "Now listen, you rich people, weep and wail…"

What dangers come with wealth, and how can we honor God with our resources?

- **Temporary Nature of Riches:** Earthly wealth is fleeting and can lead to pride and self-sufficiency if we rely on it rather than on God. Money itself is not evil, but placing our trust in it instead of God leads to spiritual downfall.

Matthew 6:19-21 – "Do not store up for yourselves treasures on earth, where moths and vermin destroy, and where thieves break in and steal. But store up for yourselves treasures in heaven, where moths and vermin do not destroy, and where thieves do not break in and steal. For where your treasure is, there your heart will be also."

1st Timothy 6:9-10 – "Those who want to get rich fall into temptation and a trap and into many foolish and harmful desires that plunge people into ruin and destruction. For the love of money is the root of all kinds of evil. Some people, eager for money, have wandered from the faith and pierced themselves with many griefs."

- **Call to Generosity:** True discipleship involves **using our resources to bless others** and invest in eternal treasures. We are called to give freely as God has given to us.

2nd Corinthians 9:6-7 – "Whoever sows sparingly will also reap sparingly, and whoever sows generously will also reap generously.

Each of you should give what you have decided in your heart to give, not reluctantly or under compulsion, for God loves a cheerful giver."

Proverbs 11:24-25 – "One person gives freely, yet gains even more; another withholds unduly, but comes to poverty. A generous person will prosper; whoever refreshes others will be refreshed."

- **Accountability:** God holds us **accountable** for how we manage what He has entrusted to us. A **generous heart** reflects God's character and pleases Him.

Luke 12:15 – "Then he said to them, 'Watch out! Be on your guard against all kinds of greed; life does not consist in an abundance of possessions.'"

Hebrews 13:16 – "And do not forget to do good and to share with others, for with such sacrifices God is pleased."

James 5:4–6 – "Look! The wages you failed to pay the workers…"

How can we ensure that we act justly in our financial dealings and treatment of others?

- **Ethical Stewardship:** As believers, we must **treat financial matters with integrity**, ensuring fairness and justice in all business and personal dealings. Honest stewardship reflects God's righteousness.

Proverbs 22:16 – "One who oppresses the poor to increase his wealth and one who gives gifts to the rich—both come to poverty."

Leviticus 19:13 – "Do not defraud or rob your neighbor. Do not hold back the wages of a hired worker overnight."

- **Compassionate Action:** We honor God by caring for those who are **economically vulnerable**, ensuring that they receive what is rightfully theirs. God calls us to use our resources to **uplift others, not exploit them**.

Proverbs 14:31 – "Whoever oppresses the poor shows contempt for their Maker, but whoever is kind to the needy honors God."

Deuteronomy 24:14-15 – "Do not take advantage of a hired worker who is poor and needy, whether that worker is a fellow Israelite or a foreigner residing in one of your towns. Pay them their wages each day before sunset because they are poor and are counting on it. Otherwise they may cry to the Lord against you, and you will be guilty of sin."

- **Reflecting God's Justice:** We must commit to practices that honor God's **standards of fairness and equity**, using our resources to **serve and bless others** rather than oppress them.

Micah 6:8 – "He has shown you, O mortal, what is good. And what does the Lord require of you? To act justly and to love mercy and to walk humbly with your God."

Luke 3:11 – "John answered, 'Anyone who has two shirts should share with the one who has none, and anyone who has food should do the same.'"

Session 10 - Key Summary Points

1. **James 5:1–3 – "Now listen, you rich people, weep and wail..."**

- James warns wealthy oppressors that their riches will not save them but will instead testify against them.
- Hoarding wealth and prioritizing material possessions over righteousness leads to corruption and judgment.
- The pursuit of wealth without regard for God or justice will result in destruction and misery.

2. **James 5:4–6 – "Look! The wages you failed to pay the workers..."**

- Injustice and exploitation of workers cry out to God, who hears and will act in judgment.
- The wealthy have lived in luxury and self-indulgence, ignoring the needs of others and even condemning the innocent.
- James warns that God sees injustice, and those who oppress others will ultimately face divine judgment.

A. Examine Where Your Treasure Is Stored

James warns about wealth that is "corroded," not because it's inherently evil, but because it was stored up selfishly. Start by asking: *Is my treasure serving God—or serving me?*

Cross-reference: Matthew 6:19–21 – "Do not store up for yourselves treasures on earth... For where your treasure is, there your heart will be also."

B. Recognize the True Owner of All Things

We are stewards, not owners. God entrusts resources to us not just for personal comfort but to advance His kingdom and care for others.

Cross-reference: Psalm 24:1 – "The earth is the Lord's, and everything in it…"

C. Break Free from Hoarding and Step into Giving

Generosity is a spiritual discipline that breaks the grip of materialism. Begin by giving intentionally, consistently, and cheerfully—even in small ways.

Cross-reference: 2 Corinthians 9:7 – "God loves a cheerful giver."

D. Be Aware of Economic Justice

James warns against exploiting others for personal gain. We must consider: *Are we living and working in ways that honor God's justice and righteousness?*

Cross-reference: Micah 6:8 – "What does the Lord require of you? To act justly and to love mercy…"

E. Seek First the Kingdom

Jesus reminds us not to worry about things but to "seek first His kingdom and His righteousness…" Kingdom-first living aligns our financial goals with eternal priorities.

Cross-reference: Colossians 3:2 – "Set your minds on things above, not on earthly things."

Closing Question:

"In what ways can you use your resources—whether financial, time, or talents—to honor God and serve others rather than storing up treasures for yourself?"

Challenge

- List what you own that you tend to "cling to." Ask God: "Am I trusting this more than You?"
- Start a **generosity journal** where you track not only what you give but also how God blesses others (and you) through it.
- Look around your community: Who could benefit from your time, talent, or treasure?

Struggle: Avoiding materialism.

Practical Steps:

- Regularly give to those in need.
- Simplify possessions and focus on eternal treasures.
- Examine spending habits in light of God's kingdom.

Conclusion:

James issues a strong warning against those who hoard wealth, exploit others, and place their trust in riches. The problem is not wealth itself but the misuse of wealth—hoarding instead of generosity, oppression instead of fairness. God calls us to be faithful stewards of our resources, using them to bless others rather than serve selfish interests.

Wealth is temporary, but our character and actions have eternal consequences. Instead of pursuing riches at the expense of justice and compassion, we should seek to honor God with what we have, using our blessings to serve Him and others.

Key Reflection:

Are we using our resources for God's glory or only for ourselves? Let's examine our attitudes toward wealth and commit to being faithful stewards, generous givers, and just in all our dealings.

Closing Prayer:

Lord, You are our true treasure. Keep us from the snare of materialism and selfish gain. Teach us to steward our resources wisely and generously. Help us to seek Your kingdom first and to use what we have to bring justice, mercy, and hope to others. We choose to trust You as our provider. In Jesus' name, Amen.

Session 11

James 5:7–12 – What does it mean to persevere and be blessed through suffering?

Endurance in the face of suffering is one of the hallmarks of a mature faith. James encourages us to remain steadfast, drawing inspiration from the farmer, Job, and the prophets, who endured hardships with patience and faith. This session will help us see that perseverance through trials leads to blessings. Let us reflect on how God uses suffering to strengthen our faith and shape us into the image of Christ.

Session 11: James 5:7–12

- James 5:7–8: "Be patient, then, brothers and sisters…"
- James 5:9–12: "Don't grumble against one another, brothers and sisters…"

7 Be patient, then, brothers and sisters, until the Lord's coming. See how the farmer waits for the land to yield its valuable crop, patiently waiting for the autumn and spring rains. **8** You too, be patient and stand firm, because the Lord's coming is near. **9** Don't grumble against each other, brothers and sisters, or you will be judged. The Judge is standing at the door! **10** Brothers and sisters, as an example of patience in the face of suffering, take the prophets who spoke in the name of the Lord. **11** As you know, we count as blessed those who have persevered. You have heard of Job's perseverance and have seen what the Lord finally brought about. The Lord is full of compassion and mercy. **12** Above all, my brothers and sisters, do not

swear—not by heaven or by earth or by anything else. All you need to say is a simple "Yes" or "No." Otherwise, you will be condemned.

James 5:7–8 – "Be patient, then, brothers and sisters…"

Why is patience crucial in the Christian life, especially in times of suffering?

- **Trust in God's Timing:** Patience demonstrates our **trust in God's perfect timing**, even when immediate outcomes are not evident. Waiting on the Lord deepens our faith and reliance on Him.

Ecclesiastes 3:1 – "There is a time for everything, and a season for every activity under the heavens."

Psalm 37:7 – "Be still before the Lord and wait patiently for him; do not fret when people succeed in their ways, when they carry out their wicked schemes."

- **Endurance Through Trials:** Patience builds **endurance**, enabling us to withstand difficulties with a hopeful spirit. Trials shape our character and strengthen our faith.

Romans 5:3-4 – "Not only so, but we also glory in our sufferings, because we know that suffering produces perseverance; perseverance, character; and character, hope."

Isaiah 40:31 – "But those who hope in the Lord will renew their strength. They will soar on wings like eagles; they will run and not grow weary, they will walk and not be faint."

- **Witness to Others:** Our patience in suffering serves as a **powerful testimony** to others of God's sustaining power and faithfulness. A patient heart reflects God's peace even in hardship.

Matthew 5:16 – "In the same way, let your light shine before others, that they may see your good deeds and glorify your Father in heaven."

Hebrews 10:36 – "You need to persevere so that when you have done the will of God, you will receive what he has promised."

James 5:9–12 – "Don't grumble against one another…"

How can we cultivate a spirit of contentment and avoid grumbling in difficult times?

- **Positive Focus:** Instead of dwelling on hardship, we should **concentrate on God's faithfulness** and the blessings in our lives. Gratitude helps shift our perspective.

Philippians 4:8 – "Finally, brothers and sisters, whatever is true, whatever is noble, whatever is right, whatever is pure, whatever is lovely, whatever is admirable—if anything is excellent or praiseworthy—think about such things."

1ˢᵗ Thessalonians 5:16-18 – "Rejoice always, pray continually, give thanks in all circumstances; for this is God's will for you in Christ Jesus."

- **Community Support:** Encouraging one another and **building a supportive community** helps prevent bitterness and promotes unity.

Hebrews 10:24-25 – "And let us consider how we may spur one another on toward love and good deeds, not giving up meeting together, as some are in the habit of doing, but encouraging one another—and all the more as you see the Day approaching."

Galatians 6:2 – "Carry each other's burdens, and in this way you will fulfill the law of Christ."

- **Mindful Speech:** Practicing **self-control** with our words allows us to **speak life and encouragement** even in tough situations rather than adding negativity.

Ephesians 4:29 – "Do not let any unwholesome talk come out of your mouths, but only what is helpful for building others up according to their needs, that it may benefit those who listen."

Proverbs 18:21 – "The tongue has the power of life and death, and those who love it will eat its fruit."

Session 11 - Key Summary Points

1. **James 5:7–8 – "Be patient, then, brothers and sisters..."**

- Believers are encouraged to be patient and stand firm as they wait for the Lord's return.
- The example of a farmer waiting for the harvest reminds us that spiritual growth and God's timing require patience.
- We must remain steadfast in our faith, trusting that God is working even when we do not see immediate results.

2. **James 5:9–12 – "Don't grumble against one another, brothers and sisters..."**

- Avoid complaining and grumbling about others, as this leads to division and invites God's judgment.
- Perseverance is key—James points to Job's example of enduring suffering while trusting God.

- Be truthful and trustworthy in your speech—let your "yes" be yes and your "no" be no—so that your words reflect integrity.

A. Embrace the Purpose of Suffering

James uses the example of a farmer to highlight patient endurance. The farmer waits for the crops to grow, trusting that the process is working, even when there's no immediate visible change. Similarly, our trials have a purpose: they develop endurance, maturity, and a deeper reliance on God.

Cross-reference: Romans 5:3–4 – "We also glory in our sufferings, because we know that suffering produces perseverance; perseverance, character; and character, hope."

B. Follow the Examples of the Faithful

James encourages us to look up to Job and the prophets as models of steadfast faith. Job endured incredible suffering but remained faithful, and in the end, he was blessed. God allows us to be tested, but He also promises to bless those who endure.

Cross-reference: Hebrews 12:1–2 – "Let us run with perseverance the race marked out for us, fixing our eyes on Jesus…"

C. Strengthen Your Heart in Hope

James calls us to "strengthen our hearts" because the Lord's coming is near. When we endure with a mindset focused on eternal hope, our trials seem more bearable because they are temporary. Hope fuels perseverance, and it reminds us that God has not abandoned us.

Cross-reference: 2 Corinthians 4:17 – "For our light and momentary troubles are achieving for us an eternal glory that far outweighs them all."

D. Avoid Grumbling and Trust God's Timing

James warns against grumbling against one another, which can lead to division and bitterness. Instead of complaining, we are to trust God's perfect timing, knowing that He is working all things for our good and His glory. Patience and trust in His plan will keep our hearts at peace.

Cross-reference: Philippians 2:14 – "Do everything without grumbling or arguing..."

E. Live with Integrity and Honesty

James also advises us to be careful with our speech, avoiding oaths, which can reflect impatience or lack of trust in God's promises. Our words should reflect our trust in God and His ability to deliver.

Cross-reference: Matthew 5:37 – "Let your 'Yes' be 'Yes,' and your 'No,' 'No'; anything beyond this comes from the evil one."

Closing Question:

"How can you practice patience and perseverance in your current season of life, trusting in God's timing and remaining steadfast in your faith?"

Challenge

- Examine your current struggles: How might they be developing perseverance and character in your life?
- Keep a "faith journal" to reflect on moments when you've experienced God's strength during hard times.

- Consider Job's response to suffering: He said, "Though He slay me, yet will I hope in Him." (Job 13:15). How can you model this hope in your own life?

Struggle: Persevering through suffering.

Practical Steps:

- Meditate on scriptures about endurance (Romans 5:3-5, 2 Corinthians 4:16-18).
- Join a small group for support.
- Keep a testimony journal of God's faithfulness.

Conclusion:

Patience is not just waiting—it's trusting God's timing and remaining steadfast in faith even when circumstances are difficult. James encourages us to look to the farmer, the prophets, and Job as examples of endurance. Their perseverance reminds us that God is faithful, even in the waiting.

Complaining and grumbling are easy in tough times, but James urges us to guard our words and trust in God's justice. Our endurance in suffering is a powerful testimony of faith, showing the world that our hope is not in temporary relief but in God's eternal promises.

Key Reflection:

Are we patiently trusting God in our trials, or are we growing weary and bitter? Let's choose to endure with faith, hope, and an unwavering trust in God's goodness and timing.

Closing Prayer:

God of patience, thank You for the examples of endurance found in Scripture. Help us to wait upon You with faith, especially when answers seem far away. Strengthen us like the farmer, like Job, like the prophets who trusted You through hardship. May our yes be yes and our no be no, always reflecting Your character. In Christ we pray, Amen.

Session 12

James 5:13–20 – Where & when does prayer play a part in your life?

Prayer is not just a ritual or a reaction to crisis—it is a lifestyle of dependence on God. James calls us to pray in all circumstances: in joy, in suffering, and in sickness. He highlights the power of fervent prayer and its role in restoring and healing. In this final session, we will reflect on the importance of prayer in our daily lives and how it can bring about transformation in our hearts and in the lives of others. Let's commit to deepening our prayer life as we seek God's will in every moment.

Session 12: James 5:13–20

- James 5:13–16: "Is anyone among you in trouble? Let them pray…"
- James 5:17–20: "Elijah was a human being, even as we are…"

13 Is anyone among you in trouble? Let them pray. Is anyone happy? Let them sing songs of praise. **14** Is anyone among you sick? Let them call the elders of the church to pray over them and anoint them with oil in the name of the Lord. **15** And the prayer offered in faith will make the sick person well; the Lord will raise them up. If they have sinned, they will be forgiven. **16** Therefore, confess your sins to each other and pray for each other so that you may be healed. The prayer of a righteous person is powerful and effective. **17** Elijah was a human being, even as we are. He prayed earnestly that it would not rain, and it did not rain on the land for three and a half years. **18** Again he prayed, and the heavens gave rain, and the earth produced its crops. **19** My brothers and sisters, if one of you should wander from the truth and someone should bring that person back, **20** remember this: Whoever turns a sinner from the error of their way will save them from death and cover over a multitude of sins.

James 5:13–16 – "Is anyone among you in trouble? Let them pray…"

How does prayer strengthen our faith and foster community?

- **Personal Connection**: Prayer is a direct line to God, deepening our personal relationship and reliance on Him. It aligns our hearts with His will.

Philippians 4:6-7 – "Do not be anxious about anything, but in every situation, by prayer and petition, with thanksgiving, present your requests to God. And the peace of God, which transcends all understanding, will guard your hearts and your minds in Christ Jesus."

Psalm 145:18 – "The Lord is near to all who call on him, to all who call on him in truth."

- **Healing and Restoration**: Through prayer, we invite God's healing into our lives—both physically and spiritually. Prayer is a powerful tool for restoration.

2ⁿᵈ Chronicles 7:14 – "If my people, who are called by my name, will humble themselves and pray and seek my face and turn from their wicked ways, then I will hear from heaven, and I will forgive their sin and will heal their land."

Mark 11:24 – "Therefore I tell you, whatever you ask for in prayer, believe that you have received it, and it will be yours."

- **Corporate Support:** Praying together creates a bond within the community, fostering mutual support and accountability.

Matthew 18:19-20 – "Again, truly I tell you that if two of you on earth agree about anything they ask for, it will be done for them by my Father in heaven. For where two or three gather in my name, there am I with them."

Acts 2:42 – "They devoted themselves to the apostles' teaching and to fellowship, to the breaking of bread and to prayer."

James 5:17–20 – "Elijah was a human being, even as we are…"

How does Elijah's example inspire us to pray with boldness and faith?

- **Realistic Humanity:** Elijah's humanity shows that even those who walk closely with God face challenges, yet God honors their earnest prayers.

1st Kings 19:4 – "He came to a broom bush, sat down under it and prayed that he might die. 'I have had enough, Lord,' he said. 'Take my life; I am no better than my ancestors.'" (Elijah experienced deep discouragement, showing his humanity.)

Hebrews 4:15-16 – "For we do not have a high priest who is unable to empathize with our weaknesses, but we have one who has been tempted in every way, just as we are—yet he did not sin. Let us then approach God's throne of grace with confidence so that we may receive mercy and find grace to help us in our time of need."

- **Bold Faith:** Elijah's example encourages us to pray boldly, trusting that God can work miracles in our lives as well.

1ˢᵗ Kings 18:36-38 – "At the time of sacrifice, the prophet Elijah stepped forward and prayed: 'Lord, the God of Abraham, Isaac and Israel, let it be known today that you are God in Israel and that I am your servant and have done all these things at your command. Answer me, Lord, answer me, so these people will know that you, Lord, are God, and that you are turning their hearts back again.' Then the fire of the Lord fell and burned up the sacrifice, the wood, the stones and the soil, and also licked up the water in the trench."

Matthew 21:21-22 – "Jesus replied, 'Truly I tell you, if you have faith and do not doubt, not only can you do what was done to the fig tree, but also you can say to this mountain, "Go, throw yourself into the sea," and it will be done. If you believe, you will receive whatever you ask for in prayer."'

- **Restoration Power:** The narrative of Elijah highlights the transformative power of prayer to bring about restoration and change in difficult circumstances.

Luke 1:37 – "For no word from God will ever fail."

Jeremiah 33:3 – "'Call to me and I will answer you and tell you great and unsearchable things you do not know.'"

Session 12 - Key Summary Points

1. **James 5:13–16 – "Is anyone among you in trouble? Let them pray..."**

- Prayer should be our first response in all situations—whether we are suffering, joyful, or sick.
- The elders of the church are encouraged to pray over the sick, anointing them with oil as an act of faith.
- Confession and prayer within the community bring healing, both physically and spiritually.
- The prayer of a righteous person is powerful and effective.

2. **James 5:17–20 – "Elijah was a human being, even as we are…"**

- James uses Elijah as an example of how fervent prayer can bring about extraordinary results.
- We are called to intercede for others and seek to restore those who have wandered from the truth.
- Bringing someone back to faith covers a multitude of sins and aligns with God's desire for restoration.

A. Pray in Every Season of Life

James reminds us to turn to prayer no matter what we're facing— whether in moments of joy, pain, or need. Prayer is not just a response to crisis but a vital part of our daily lives, whether we are celebrating God's goodness or struggling with hardship.

- In joy: Expressing gratitude and praise (Psalm 100:4).
- In suffering: Turning to God for comfort and strength (Psalm 34:18).
- In need: Asking for wisdom and provision (Matthew 7:7-8).

Cross-reference: Philippians 4:6–7 – "Do not be anxious about anything, but in every situation, by prayer and petition, with thanksgiving, present your requests to God."

B. Be Bold and Persistent in Prayer

James highlights the strength of fervent prayer, pointing to Elijah as proof that sincere, persistent prayer has the power to bring real change—and that same call to pray with bold faith applies to us today.

Elijah's example: He prayed earnestly that it wouldn't rain, and it didn't for three and a half years. When he prayed again, the rain came (1 Kings 17–18). His prayers were bold, specific, and in line with God's will.

Cross-reference: Matthew 7:7–8 – "Ask and it will be given to you; seek and you will find; knock and the door will be opened to you."

C. Confession and Healing in Prayer

James points to the importance of confession and healing. When we bring our struggles before God, we invite His healing—physically, emotionally, and spiritually. Prayer should be a safe place where we lay down our burdens, confess our sins, and receive restoration.

- Confession of sins: Not just asking for forgiveness but also seeking restoration and healing.
- Accountability: Prayer can also involve confessing to one another, building up accountability, and mutual support.

Cross-reference: 1 John 1:9 – "If we confess our sins, He is faithful and just and will forgive us our sins and purify us from all unrighteousness."

D. Partnering in Prayer for Others

James calls us to pray for one another and to seek restoration for those who have strayed. Prayer isn't just personal—it has a communal aspect. We are called to pray for the restoration of others:

whether they are in sin, suffering, or simply in need of encouragement.

- Intercession: Taking the time to pray for others' needs, trusting that God will work in their lives.
- Restoration: Praying not just for physical healing but for spiritual renewal and reconciliation.

Cross-reference: 1 Timothy 2:1–2 – "I urge, then, first of all, that petitions, prayers, intercession, and thanksgiving be made for all people..."

E. Trusting God's Sovereignty in Prayer

Though God listens to our prayers, He knows what is best for us. Therefore, while we ask, we trust that He will answer according to His will and in His perfect timing. Prayer aligns our hearts with God's purposes and reminds us that He is in control.

Cross-reference: Romans 8:28 – "And we know that in all things God works for the good of those who love Him, who have been called according to His purpose."

Closing Question:

"How can you become more intentional in prayer—both for yourself and for others—and play a role in restoring those who have drifted from faith?"

Challenge:

- **Examine your prayer life:** Are you quick to pray in all circumstances or only in times of need? How can you cultivate a more consistent, joyful, and expectant prayer life?
- **Pray boldly and persistently:** Choose one area of your life or the life of someone you know where you need to pray

persistently for God's intervention or restoration. Commit to praying about this regularly.

- **Confess and seek healing:** Take time to confess any unspoken burdens and invite healing into your life, knowing that God's grace is abundant.

Struggle: Making prayer a priority.

Practical Steps:

- Set specific times each day for prayer.
- Keep a prayer journal to track requests and answers.
- Engage in corporate prayer and intercession.

Conclusion:

James closes his letter by emphasizing the power of prayer in every season—in suffering, in joy, in sickness, and in restoration. Prayer connects us to God's power, brings healing, and strengthens our faith. The example of Elijah shows us that fervent prayer can bring transformation.

Additionally, we are called to support one another in prayer, confessing our sins and lifting each other up. The Christian life is not meant to be lived in isolation—we are a family, called to encourage, restore, and stand in the gap for one another.

Key Reflection:

Are we making prayer a central part of our lives? This week, let's commit to being intentional in prayer—seeking God daily, interceding for others, and believing in the power of prayer to bring change.

Closing Prayer:

Faithful God, thank You for the gift of prayer. Whether in joy or sorrow, health or weakness, may we always turn to You. Teach us to pray with expectation, to intercede for others, and to believe for restoration. Use us to bring healing, hope, and truth to those who wander. Let prayer be the heartbeat of our daily walk with You. In Jesus' powerful name, Amen.

Conclusion Session: Living Out the Book of James

As we come to the conclusion of our study through the Book of James, we are reminded that faith is not merely something we profess but something we live out every day. James has challenged us to live with authenticity—embracing trials, controlling our speech, living with humility, and putting our faith into action. This letter has not only stirred our hearts but also called us to a life of practical obedience, one that reflects Christ in all things.

In this final session, we will take time to reflect on the truths we've uncovered and consider how to apply them actively in our lives. We'll look at how we can continue to endure, live justly, seek wisdom, and, most importantly, depend on God in every circumstance. Let this time be an opportunity for us to renew our commitment to be doers of the Word, not just hearers, and to live out our faith in every decision, relationship, and action.

Let's commit ourselves to living the teachings of James, allowing them to shape our lives into a testimony of God's love, power, and grace. May our faith be one that stands firm, shows mercy, and leads others to the hope of Christ.

Key Themes to Take Away:

1. **Trials Build Endurance** *(James 1:2-4)* – Every hardship is an opportunity for growth in faith and character.

2. **Faith is More Than Words** *(James 2:14-26)* – Genuine faith results in action.

3. **Wisdom from Above** *(James 3:17-18)* – True wisdom is humble, peace-loving, and bears good fruit.

4. **Submitting to God** *(James 4:7-10)* – A surrendered heart resists the devil and draws near to God.

5. **The Power of Prayer** *(James 5:16-18)* – A righteous person's prayer is powerful and effective.

A. Embrace Trials as Opportunities for Growth

- **Action Step:** View challenges and hardships not as obstacles but as opportunities for spiritual growth. Remember that perseverance through trials refines your character and strengthens your faith.

- **Example:** When facing a difficulty, stop to pray and ask God to show you how He might be using this situation to mature your faith.

Key Insight from James 1:2-4: "Consider it pure joy, my brothers and sisters, whenever you face trials of many kinds, because you know that the testing of your faith produces perseverance."

B. Be Doers of the Word, Not Just Hearers

- **Action Step:** Don't just listen to God's Word; apply it in your life. Let your faith be visible through your actions and choices.

- **Example:** When you hear a scripture that challenges you (such as loving your neighbor), make an intentional plan to act on it this week.

Key Insight from James 1:22: "Do not merely listen to the word, and so deceive yourselves. Do what it says."

C. Guard Your Speech

- **Action Step:** Take control over what you say. Use your words to encourage, build up, and speak life into others. Practice speaking with kindness and wisdom.

- **Example:** When you feel frustration building, pause and ask the Holy Spirit to help you speak with grace and truth.

Key Insight from James 3:9-10: "With the tongue, we praise our Lord and Father, and with it we curse human beings, who have been made in God's likeness. Out of the same mouth come praise and cursing. My brothers and sisters, this should not be."

D. Live Out Your Faith Through Actions

- **Action Step:** Put your faith into action. Whether it's helping someone in need, serving in your community, or showing kindness, allow your faith to be demonstrated through deeds.

- **Example:** When you hear of someone struggling financially, look for ways to practically meet their needs, whether through prayer, support, or resources.

Key Insight from James 2:17: "In the same way, faith by itself, if it is not accompanied by action, is dead."

E. Seek God's Wisdom Above Worldly Wisdom

- **Action Step:** When making decisions, seek God's wisdom first, trusting that He will guide you. Reflect on James' distinction between godly wisdom, which brings peace, and worldly wisdom, which can lead to conflict.

- **Example:** Before making a major decision (career change, financial investment, relationship), take time to pray, seek counsel, and ask God for wisdom.

Key Insight from James 3:17: "But the wisdom that comes from heaven is first of all pure; then peace-loving, considerate, submissive, full of mercy and good fruit, impartial and sincere."

F. Live with Humility and Submit to God

- **Action Step:** Resist the temptation to exalt yourself or to rely on your strength. Submit to God's will in all areas of your life, and trust His timing and plan for you.

- **Example:** When you face opposition or challenges, choose to humble yourself before God and trust that He will lift you up in due time.

Key Insight from James 4:10: "Humble yourselves before the Lord, and he will lift you up."

G. Pray in All Circumstances

- **Action Step:** Cultivate a habit of prayer. Pray in times of joy, sorrow, need, and thanksgiving. Be persistent and specific in your prayers, trusting in God's power to bring change.

- **Example:** When something unexpected happens, take a moment to pray and ask God for His perspective and help, even in small matters.

Key Insight from James 5:13-16: "Is anyone among you in trouble? Let them pray. Is anyone happy? Let them sing songs of praise."

H. Repent and Restore When Necessary

- **Action Step:** If you recognize areas in your life where you've strayed from God's will, repent and seek His restoration. Pray for others who need help in returning to the truth.

- **Example:** If you've been harboring unforgiveness or pride, confess it to God and take steps to reconcile with those you've wronged.

Key Insight from James 5:19-20: "My brothers and sisters, if one of you should wander from the truth and someone should bring that person back, remember this: Whoever turns a sinner from the error of their way will save them from death and cover over a multitude of sins."

Final Reflection Questions:

- What lesson from James challenged you the most?

- How has this study changed the way you live out your faith?

- What action steps will you take to grow in obedience to God?

James calls us to an active faith—one that is proven by endurance, obedience, love, wise speech, and dependence on God. Let us commit to being doers of the Word, not just hearers *(James 1:22)*.

Finally, James ends his letter with a call to restore one another in love *(James 5:19-20)*. May this study inspire us to not only grow personally but also to encourage and strengthen those around us.

Closing Prayer:

Heavenly Father, we thank You for the wisdom and conviction found in the Book of James. You have called us to live out our faith with endurance, love, and action. Help us to be doers of Your Word, not just hearers. Strengthen us through trials, guide us in wisdom, and fill our hearts with Your Spirit. May our words, our deeds, and our lives reflect the love of Christ. In Jesus' name, we pray. Amen.